D1080622

Instant

Games

for Children

Susan L. Lingo

101 fun-filled children's games

To my mom, Peggy, and her loving, playful heart.

Text copyright © Susan L. Lingo 2009
Illustrations copyright © Rebecca Thornburgh 2009
The author asserts the moral right
to be identified as the author of this work

Published by
The Bible Reading Fellowship
15 The Chambers, Vineyard
Abingdon OX14 3FE
United Kingdom
Tel: +44 (0)1865 319700
Email: enquiries@brf.org.uk
Website: www.brf.org.uk

ISBN 978 1 84101 591 0
First published 1995
Group Publishing, Inc.
Dept. BK
Box 481
Loveland
CO 80539.2008
USA

UK edition first published 2009
10 9 8 7 6 5 4 3 2 1 0

Printed in Singapore by Craft Print International Ltd

Contents

Introduction

The key to game confidence

Children love to play games. But coming up with new and exciting games to play with your children is often frustrating, and collecting game equipment can be costly and time consuming. Not any more! *Instant Games for Children* is a collection of fast-paced, fun-to-play games for every child in your group. And with the handy game bag, all playing pieces are at your fingertips any time, anywhere.

The key to successfully playing games with children may be summed up in two words: *game confidence*! When you are familiar with a myriad exciting games and have the equipment to play them, games can be an enriching time of fellowship for everyone.

Why play games?

No children's programme can be built on games alone—yet the effective use of game-time helps nurture many positive benefits, including:

❖ Community building
❖ Getting to know each other
❖ Burning excess energy to help children refocus
❖ Strengthening teamwork and cooperation
❖ Creating a welcoming, positive atmosphere

Games that foster cooperation, instead of competition, help children feel accepted and successful with peers and leaders. The games included in *Instant Games for Children* are cooperative and not based on 'winners' and 'losers': everyone is a winner in the good-time department!

How Instant Games work

Each game in *Instant Games for Children* uses an item from the handy game bag, which is quickly assembled by 'shopping' your home, discount stores, garage sales, other church members, or closing-down sales. Here are the simple items you'll need to play 101 different games:

- ❖ A roll of masking tape
- ❖ Two ping-pong balls
- ❖ Two rulers
- ❖ A playground ball
- ❖ A foam ball
- ❖ Six plastic tumblers or cups
- ❖ Six circular foam coasters (or discs)
- ❖ Two skipping ropes
- ❖ A bag of balloons
- ❖ Two cotton headscarves
- ❖ A kitchen timer
- ❖ A colour cube and a number cube (which will be explained later)

Assemble these simple, inexpensive items in a pillowcase, laundry basket, box, or bin bag, and you'll be ready any time you or your children say, 'Let's play a game!'

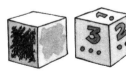 To make the colour and number cubes, simply cover two small square boxes with white self-adhesive shelf paper. For the colour cube, use permanent markers to colour the sides red, yellow, green, and blue. You'll use two colours twice. For the number cube, use a marker to add numerals and dots to represent numbers from one to four. Again, you'll use two numbers twice.

Have fun!

That's all there is to it! You are now ready to energize your children by offering them a wonderful selection of games that are sure to become group favourites. And best of all, these games will travel with your group inside, outside, to the large hall, on picnics, and to away days.

So go wild. Be daring. And have fun playing games with your children as you all share in the joy of friendship and fun!

 **Taxi! Taxi!**

Get ready...

Group size: Eight or more
Best for ages: 5–11s
Playing time: 15 minutes
Energy level: Medium
Items needed: The number cube and a cup

Get set...

Aim of the game
Find a matching taxi and be the first pair to snatch the cup.

Go!

How to play
Set the cup at one end of the playing area and gather children at the opposite end. Form two groups and designate one group as the taxis and the other as the passengers. Have the two groups stand a few feet apart. Direct the taxis to secretly number off by fours.

What to say
It's a rainy day, and there aren't many taxis for people to ride in! I'll roll the number cube and call out, 'Taxi number two!' (or whatever number is rolled). Passengers, race to find a taxi that matches that number by asking taxis their numbers. Then taxi and passenger can lock arms and rush to pick up the cup.

After each round, have the taxis secretly renumber themselves. When you have played a few rounds, swap roles so the passengers become the taxis and vice versa.

Walk the line

Get ready...

Group size: Eight or more
Best for ages: 6–11s
Playing time: Ten minutes
Energy level: Medium to low
Items needed: The playground ball and two cotton headscarves

Get set...

Aim of the game

As your partner deflects the ball, safely deliver a headscarf from one end of the line to the other.

Go!

How to play

Form two lines and stand facing each other, three feet apart. Lay the scarves at the two ends (see diagram). Hand the playground ball to a child in the middle of one line. Designate one line the 'guards' and the other line the 'grabbers'. The children opposite each other at the ends of the lines are partners.

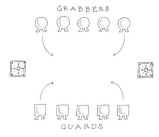

GRABBERS

GUARDS

What to say

When I say 'go', the partners from the ends of each line will go to the headscarves. The grabbers will each pick up a scarf and walk between the lines while you try to tag them with the ball. Guards can block the shots to keep their partners safe. If the grabber makes it to the opposite end of the line without being tagged, he or she sets the scarf down and both partners go to the middle of the lines to wait for their next turn. If a grabber is tagged, the grabber and guard aren't eligible to walk the line again, but they can return to the line to help tag others. Then the next partners on the ends walk the line.

Have pairs take turns walking the line until there's only one pair that hasn't been tagged.

Panic pass

Get ready...

Group size: Any
Best for ages: 6–11s
Playing time: 15 minutes
Energy level: Medium
Items needed: All game items

Get set...

Aim of the game

Don't get caught without an item when the passing frenzy stops!

Go!

How to play

Sit in a circle on the floor. Choose one child to be the 'roller' and give him or her the colour cube. Instruct the roller to sit in the centre of the circle. Let each player choose one game item to hold.

 What to say

This is a speedy passing game! We'll start passing the items around the circle to the right. Be sure you're holding only one item at a time. The roller will roll the colour cube and call out the colour rolled. If the colour is blue, we'll reverse the passing direction; if the colour is yellow, we'll slow down; if the colour is green, we'll speed up the passing; and if the colour is red, we'll stop. If we stop, and you're caught without an item or with more than one item, come to the centre and help the roller. We'll remove an item for each person who comes to the centre. Let's play until there are only two players left in the circle.

Begin passing items to the right. Be sure to remove an item each time someone goes to the centre of the circle. (There should always be one item for each person in the circle.)

Inside tip

Help children remember the colour code by comparing it to traffic lights. Red is stop, yellow is slow down, and green is go, or speed up.

Tightrope toss

Get ready...

Group size: Six or more
Best for ages: 5–11s
Playing time: Ten minutes
Energy level: Medium
Items needed: The foam ball, the playground ball and the masking tape

Get set...

Aim of the game
Walk the 'tightrope' while throwing and catching the balls.

Go!

How to play
Create a five-foot square 'tightrope' on the floor using masking tape. If you have six to eight children, make a triangular tightrope. Direct the children to line up around the tightrope. (Make sure there are children on every side of the tightrope.) Hand two children the balls.

What to say

In this death-defying circus act, you must walk the wobbly tightrope as you throw the balls to each other! If you drop a ball or step off the tightrope, come and sit in the centre. Centre people may call out directions such as 'hop', 'change direction', or 'walk backward'. Tightrope walkers must follow those directions. We'll play until there are only two tightrope walkers left.

Inside tip

Older children may enjoy walking the tightrope in pairs. Have partners link arms and walk sideways around the tightrope.

The pits

Get ready...

Group size: Eight or more
Best for ages: 7–11s
Playing time: 15 minutes
Energy level: High
Items needed: The masking tape, two skipping ropes, six cups and the playground ball

Get set...

Aim of the game

Work as a group to knock over your opponents' cups.

Go!

How to play

This game is best suited to a large hall or outside play. Divide the playing area in half with a five-foot line of masking tape. Lay each skipping rope 20 feet away from the centre line to create 'pit zones'. Set three cups at random on each side of the centre line (see diagram). Form two groups and have them stand on opposite sides of the centre line.

What to say

This game may be called 'the pits', but you'll have a great time playing! The object is to knock over the other group's cups. You may roll the playground ball with your hands to knock cups over,

and you may also block shots from hitting your cups. But each time a cup on your side is toppled, one of your players must go to the 'pit zone' on the other side. He or she stays there until someone in your group rolls the ball to him or her. Then that player may safely return to your side and set up a cup. We'll play until one side has all the cups knocked over.

> ### Inside tip
>
> Older children may enjoy using the foam ball and the playground ball simultaneously. For another twist, have children use their feet instead of their hands to roll the ball.

Splashdown!

Get ready...

Group size: Four or more
Best for ages: 5–11s
Playing time: 15 minutes per round
Energy level: High
Items needed: Two cups, two ping-pong balls, two cotton headscarves and some water

Get set...

Aim of the game

Be the astronauts with the most water in your 'splashdown' cup at the end of the game.

Go!

How to play

This game is best played outside in the summer. Make sure children are wearing clothes that can get damp from some splashy fun!

Fill two cups with water. Form two groups of 'astronauts' and hand each group a ping-pong ball and a headscarf. Direct each group to choose an astronaut to go first. Hand him or her a splashdown cup. Set a ping-pong ball in the centre of each scarf and instruct group members to hold a portion of this 'launchpad'.

What to say

Every astronaut wants a great splashdown. We'll pretend the ping-pong balls are rocket ships and launch them into orbit. Then the astronauts with the cups will race to make great splashdowns and catch the rocket ships. If you catch your rocket ship, swap places with another astronaut in your group. If you miss, try again.

Encourage children to shout group countdowns by saying, 'Three, two, one, blast off!' as they launch the ping-pong balls in the air using the headscarves.

Continue launching and catching the rocket ships until all the astronauts have made successful splashdowns. Let the group with the most water left in their cup line up first for refreshments.

> **Inside tip**
> For an indoor variation, have children launch the discs or the number and colour cubes and catch them with their hands instead of the cups.

 # Action subtraction

Get ready...

Group size: Ten or more
Best for ages: 7–11s
Playing time: Ten minutes
Energy level: Low
Item needed: The number cube

Get set...

Aim of the game
Use group strategy to subtract the 'numbers' in a number line.

Go!

How to play

Choose eight children to stand in front of the group. (You may choose ten children if your group is very large.) Help them number off from one to eight (or ten). Direct the children to hold up their assigned number using their fingers. These are the 'number children'. Have the other children find partners.

What to say

Let's play a game called 'Action subtraction'. We'll try to subtract number children until there's no one left standing in the number line. Partners will roll the number cube, then decide which number children to subtract. For example, if a two and four are rolled, number six may sit down because two plus four equals six, or numbers two and four may sit down. If there's no one to sit down with the numbers rolled, pass the number cube to the next pair.

Play until all of the number children are sitting down. Then choose new number children to take their places. Continue until everyone has been a number child at least once.

Inside tip

Older children may enjoy a special challenge. Have pairs play against each other and either add or subtract number children to prevent the other side from going out. The game ends when one side finally subtracts all the number children.

Two are better than one

Get ready...

Group size: Any
Best for ages: 5–8s
Playing time: 15 minutes
Energy level: Medium
Items needed: Two skipping ropes, a cup and two cotton
                  headscarves

Get set...

Aim of the game

Travel with your partner in a wacky way and be the first pair to snatch the cup.

Go!

How to play

Lay the skipping ropes end to end as a starting line. Place the cup 20 feet away from the starting line. Form two groups and have children find partners within their groups. (If there's an extra child, form a trio.)

What to say

Some things are easier to do when you have friends to help. You can help your partners in this game. Huddle with your partner and decide how you'll travel from the starting line to the cup. You can travel in wacky ways such as rolling over and over or hopping or standing on your partner's feet and walking. Oh, there's just one rule: You must have your legs fastened to your partner's legs with a headscarf!

When children have had a moment to decide on their mode of travel, have the first two pairs step to the starting line. Loosely tie their legs together with the headscarves. Invite everyone to say, 'Ready, set, go!' The first pair to reach the cup can hold it in the air. Continue until each pair has had a turn. Then encourage each player to give his or her partner a pat on the back for their help.

 # Triangle tangle ball

Get ready...

Group size: Eight or more
Best for ages: 6–11s
Playing time: 15 minutes
Energy level: High
Items needed: One skipping rope, six cups, two cotton headscarves, a disc and the playground ball

Get set...

Aim of the game
Travel safely around the triangle and score 'cups' for your group.

Go!

How to play
This game is best suited to outdoor play and is similar to kickball. Lay the skipping rope on the ground for home base. Set six cups beside home base. Place the headscarves 20 feet from the skipping rope at outward angles (see diagram). The skipping rope and scarves should form the points of a triangle with 20 feet between each point. Place the disc in the centre of the triangle.

Have children get into two groups: the 'fielders' and the 'kickers'. Tell the fielders to choose a 'roller' and have the roller stand on the disc while holding the playground ball. The other fielders will guard the scarves.

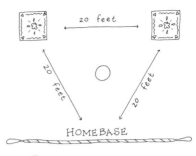

 What to say
This is a game played like baseball. In

this game, when the roller rolls you the ball, you'll kick the ball and try to run to the bases without getting tagged. On the way to home base, pick up a cup to score one point for your group. We'll swap fielders and kickers after three people are tagged out.

Continue playing until there are three outs, then fielders and kickers swap places. The game is over when all the cups have been grabbed.

 # Helping handball

Get ready...

Group size: Eight or more
Best for ages: 6–11s
Playing time: Ten minutes
Energy level: High
Items needed: The masking tape and the playground ball

Get set...

Aim of the game
Help your partner dodge the ball and be the last pair in the game.

Go!

How to play
Run a ten-foot strip of masking tape down the centre of the playing area. Form two groups and have each group stand on opposite sides of the centre line. Direct the children to find partners within their groups.

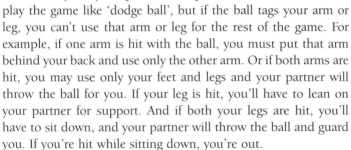

What to say
This is an exciting game, but you'll need to rely on your partner's help! We'll play the game like 'dodge ball', but if the ball tags your arm or leg, you can't use that arm or leg for the rest of the game. For example, if one arm is hit with the ball, you must put that arm behind your back and use only the other arm. Or if both arms are hit, you may use only your feet and legs and your partner will throw the ball for you. If your leg is hit, you'll have to lean on your partner for support. And if both your legs are hit, you'll have to sit down, and your partner will throw the ball and guard you. If you're hit while sitting down, you're out.

Bounce the playground ball into the playing area to begin the game. Continue playing until there's only one set of partners remaining.

Inside tip
Remind children to throw the ball at or below waist level. You may want to impose a penalty for shots above the waist, such as a two-minute timeout for the person who threw the ball.

Silly scarf

Get ready...

Group size: Any
Best for ages: 5–11s
Playing time: 15 minutes
Energy level: Low
Items needed: Two skipping ropes, a cotton headscarf and the colour cube

Get set...

Aim of the game
Be the first to snatch the colour cube in this game of giggles and grins.

Go!

How to play
Place the skipping ropes at one end of the playing area as the starting line. Choose one child to hold the headscarf and stand at least 15 feet from the starting line. Set the colour cube beside the child holding the scarf. Instruct the other children to stand on the starting line.

What to say
Laughing makes us feel great—but once you start laughing, can you stop? When the scarf is dropped, start laughing. Then walk toward the colour cube. But watch out, because when the scarf is picked up, you must stop laughing and freeze in place. No giggles—no grins! If you laugh before the scarf is dropped, you must return to the starting line and begin again. The first one to pick up the colour cube is the next scarf dropper.

Play until you have had two or three headscarf droppers. You may wish to add a different twist by having children hop or crawl to the colour cube instead of walking.

 # Belly boppin'

Get ready...

Group size: Any
Best for ages: 7–11s
Playing time: Ten minutes
Energy level: Medium
Items needed: The balloons

Get set...

Aim of the game
Be the first pair to bop 'n' pop your balloons.

Go!

How to play
Blow up and tie off a balloon for each child in your group. Have the children find partners. If there is an uneven number of children in your group, a trio will work. Distribute a balloon to each pair.

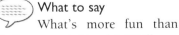 **What to say**
What's more fun than balloons and friends? We'll use

both to play this exciting game! When I say 'bop-bop-bop', tap your balloon back and forth in the air. When I say 'pop!' grab your balloon and wedge it between your partner's tummy and your own. Bop against the balloons until they pop. When your balloon pops, shout 'Bopped 'n' popped!'

After all the balloons are popped, have the children find new partners. Then repeat the game, having children wedge their balloons against their backs or knees to pop them.

Inside tip

This is a great icebreaker for kick-off parties at the beginning of the year. Provide a few more balloons and let children swap partners to pop balloons by sitting on them or stamping on them.

 Cat and mouse

Get ready...

Group size: Any
Best for ages: 5–8s
Playing time: Ten minutes
Energy level: High
Items needed: Two cotton headscarves

Get set...

Aim of the game
Grab the mouse's tail before he gets to his den.

Go!

How to play

Have the children sit or stand in a circle. Choose one child to be the mouse and hand him or her the headscarves. Direct the mouse to tuck one of the scarves inside his or her waistband or belt so it hangs down like a tail. (If the child has no waistband or belt, have the child simply hold the scarf behind them at the waist like a tail.)

What to say

This is a speedy, sneaky mouse. The rest of you are cats that like to chase mice. The mouse will walk around the circle holding a headscarf. If the mouse drops the scarf behind you, pick it up and chase the mouse. If you snatch the mouse's tail before he or she gets around the circle to your place, you're faster than a mouse! But if the mouse gets safely to your place, you become the next mouse.

Play until everyone has had a chance to chase the mouse. Instead of running each time, have children crawl, hop, walk backward, or walk heel to toe around the circle.

Cupboard clean-out

Get ready...

Group size: Eight or more
Best for ages: 6–9s
Playing time: 15 minutes
Energy level: Medium
Items needed: The masking tape, six cups, six discs, a cotton headscarf, two ping-pong balls, the number cube and the kitchen timer

25

Get set...

Aim of the game
Be the group with the cleanest 'cupboard' when time runs out.

Go!

How to play
Divide your playing area in half using a masking tape line. Form two groups and have the groups stand on opposite sides of the line. Place three cups, three discs, a headscarf, and a ping-pong ball on each side of the centre line. Set the number cube on the line.

What to say
Cleaning out cupboards is a lot of work, but in this game it's a lot of fun, too! When I begin the timer and say 'go', race to throw things out of your cupboard and over the centre line into your neighbour's cupboard. But watch out, because they'll be throwing stuff back into your cupboard just as quickly. Keep cleaning those cupboards until time runs out. Then we'll see who has the cleanest cupboard in town.

Begin the timer and say 'go'. After one round of play, form two new groups and play again. When the games are over, encourage children to give each other handshakes and say, 'You're a great cleanin' machine!'

Inside tip
Add extra excitement and 'cleaning frenzy' by challenging groups not to get caught with the number cube on their side when time runs out.

Human tug o' war

Get ready...

Group size: Eight or more
Best for ages: 9–11s
Playing time: Ten minutes
Energy level: Medium
Items needed: The masking tape and four cups

Get set...

Aim of the game
Do the 'strongman stretch' and be the first to snatch a cup.

Go!

How to play
Use the masking tape to mark off a seven-foot square on the floor, then set a cup at each corner. Place a small masking tape X in the centre of the square. Have the children find partners. Choose two pairs, and have each partner 'A' place a foot on the X and link arms. Have each partner 'B' place one arm around partner 'A''s waist (see diagram).

What to say
Put on your strongman muscles—we're going to stretch and reach in this game. When I say 'go', tug on each other and be the first pair to snatch a cup from one

of the corners. Don't let go of your partner's waist or the other pair automatically wins the round.

Continue until each pair has had a turn to pull. For older children, try using four pairs and have a four-way tug o' war (see diagram).

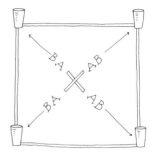

 **Minefield**

Get ready...

Group size: Any
Best for ages: 5–7s
Playing time: Ten minutes
Energy level: Medium
Items needed: A skipping rope, two cotton headscarves, six discs, six cups, the foam ball and two ping-pong balls

Get set...

Aim of the game
Work your way safely through the course without touching any obstacles.

Go!

How to play
Establish start and finish lines using a skipping rope and the headscarves. Invite children to scatter the discs, cups, foam ball,

and ping-pong balls between the lines as make-believe explosive mines. When the obstacles are all 'planted', have the children find partners and decide who'll be the 'guide' and who'll be the 'creeper'.

What to say

There are pretend mines planted all over the course. Creepers, your mission is to make it safely through the minefield by listening carefully to the directions your guide gives you. There's one rule: creepers must keep their eyes closed at all times! When you cross the finish line, creepers and guides will swap places and return to the starting line. If you bump into a mine, you and your partner must freeze in place and count to ten out loud before continuing.

If you have younger children in your group, let the creepers walk through the minefield holding the hands of their guides.

Inside tip

This game is a great reinforcement for the concepts of cooperation, communication and reliance.

 Wiggle worm

Get ready...

Group size: Any
Best for ages: 5–7s
Playing time: Ten minutes
Energy level: Medium
Items needed: Two skipping ropes and two cotton headscarves

Get set...

Aim of the game
Make a cooperative wiggling 'worm' that reaches to the finish line.

Go!

How to play
Lay the skipping ropes at one end of the playing area as the starting line. Place the headscarves at the opposite end as the finish line. Have the children form two or three groups and line up behind the starting line.

What to say
If you've ever watched wiggly worms crawl, you know they really s-t-r-e-t-c-h out! We're going to stretch our way to the finish line. When I say 'wiggle!' the first person in each worm line can get on their tummy and stretch their arms out in front. Then the next person lies in front with their feet in the hands of player one, and so on. When everyone is lying down, the person at the back of the worm line jumps up and runs to the front. Continue until your worm reaches the finish line.

Inside tip
For a fun twist, scatter a few obstacles along the way, then have the entire group create one wiggly worm to travel around the obstacles from start to finish.

 **Make a wish**

Get ready...

Group size: Up to 20
Best for ages: 5–11s
Playing time: 15 minutes
Energy level: Low
Items needed: The number cube and a game item for each child

Get set...

Aim of the game
Exercise your amazing memory skills and collect different items from other players.

Go!

How to play
Sit in a circle on the floor and have children number off by fours. Place a game item for each child in the centre and allow each one to choose an item to hold. Direct the children to hold their items up for 15 seconds and encourage them to remember who has which item. After 15 seconds, tell the children to hide the items in their laps.

Roll the number cube and call out the number rolled. Each player with that number gets to ask for an item by pointing at another player and saying, 'I wish for a [name of the item that child is holding]'. If the appointed player has the item wished for, he or she must give it to the 'wisher'. Continue until everyone has 'wished' for an item at least twice. At the end of the game, the players with the most items get to line up first for treats or drinks.

 **Partner pulley-tag**

Get ready...

Group size: Six or more
Best for ages: 5–11s
Playing time: 15 minutes
Energy level: High
Item needed: The playground ball

Get set...

Aim of the game
Tag opposing partners until only one pair is standing.

Go!

How to play
Form pairs and decide who's the 'scooper' and who's the 'thrower'. Have the pairs lock arms.

What to say
We all enjoy a good game of tag. But this game of tag has a new twist: you'll work with partners to tag others. Each partner has an important job—scoopers can only pick up the ball, and throwers can only throw it. You'll have to work cooperatively to tag others, and you must stay locked to your partner's arms. If either partner gets tagged by the ball, you both must sit down. We'll play until there's only one pair left standing. If you're tagged out, cheer the others on.

Throw the playground ball into the playing area to begin the game. Continue playing until one pair is standing. Play the game a second time, with scoopers and throwers swapping roles.

Hocus-pocus hats

Get ready...

Group size: Eight or more
Best for ages: 5–7s
Playing time: Ten minutes
Energy level: Low
Items needed: Six cups and two ping-pong balls

Get set...

Aim of the game

Hide and then seek the ping-pong ball in this simple guessing game.

Go!

How to play

Form two groups: the 'Ali' group and the 'Kazam' group. Hand each group three cups and a ping-pong ball. Tell groups to choose three people to wear the cups like hats. Then invite the groups to form huddles and secretly slide their ping-pong ball under one of their 'hats'. Tell children to hold the hats on their heads.

What to say

We'll take turns guessing where the ping-pong balls are hidden. One person from each group can remove one of their opponent's hats. If the ping-pong ball is under that hat, you may choose someone from that group to join your group. If the ping-pong ball isn't under that hat, you must join the other group. After five rounds, we'll see which group has the most members.

Before you finish playing, be sure everyone has had a chance to wear a hat at least once.

Inside tip

This is a great game to use with young children for icebreakers and beginning-of-the-year parties.

 Super racers

Get ready...

Group size: Any
Best for ages: 5–9s
Playing time: 15 minutes
Energy level: Medium
Items needed: A balloon, a disc, a cup, a cotton headscarf,
                     a ping-pong ball and the colour cube

Get set...

Aim of the game
Be the first to pass your racer around the racetrack.

Go!

How to play
Blow up and tie off the balloon. Have the children sit in a circle, and place the balloon, the disc, the cup, the headscarf, the ping-pong ball and the colour cube in the centre. Choose two children to be 'senders' and have them each pick an item to use as a 'racer'.

34

What to say

It's a fine day at the races, and you've chosen some unusual racers. We're going to speed-pass the racers around the circle, but first the senders will tell us how to pass their racers. For example, 'The [item] will be passed under your knees' or 'The [item] will be passed behind your back'. When I say 'go', senders can pass their racers in opposite directions. The racer that makes it back to the sender first will race against someone else in the next round.

Begin the game and have children pass the racers in opposite directions. Make sure the children are passing the racers in the specified manners. At the end of the first race, let the child whose racer finished second return his or her item to the centre of the circle and choose someone else to race. Continue until everyone has had a turn to race an item.

Inside tip

For extra fun, have three or four racers speeding in different directions simultaneously.

 ## Balancing act

Get ready...

Group size: Four or more
Best for ages 5–7s
Playing time: Ten minutes
Energy level: Medium
Items needed: Two cotton headscarves, six discs, six cups, two rulers and the colour and number cubes

35

Get set...

Aim of the game

Work with your partner to balance items on your head or shoulders and then walk to the finish line together.

Go!

How to play

Establish start and finish lines by placing headscarves at opposite ends of the playing area. Place the discs, the cups and the rulers behind the finish line. Have the children get into red, yellow, blue and green colour groups and find partners in their groups. Let them choose which partner will be the first balancer, then have partners stand behind the starting line.

What to say

This game is a real balancing act! I'll roll the colour and number cubes. Let's say we roll a three and the colour red. The pairs in the red group will hop to the finish line. The balancer in each pair will balance three items on his or her head and shoulders. Then the pair will return to the starting line. If any items drop, the partner without the items must pick up the fallen objects and replace them on the balancer's head or shoulders. When you reach the starting line, swap roles and return to the finish line.

Inside tip

If you have a small group, this game may be played without partners. Vary the places where items may be balanced. For example, create a balancing act with your elbows and the backs of your hands, or with your knees and your noses.

Field football

Get ready...

Group size: Six or more
Best for ages: 7–11s
Playing time: 15 minutes or longer
Energy level: High
Items needed: The playground ball, two skipping ropes, two cotton headscarves, and six cups

Get set...

Aim of the game
Using only your feet, try to knock over your opponents' cups.

Go!

How to play
Establish goal lines by placing the skipping ropes 50 feet apart. Set three cups one foot apart in front of each skipping rope. Lay the headscarves in the centre of the playing area. Form team A and team B and direct them to stand on opposite sides of the scarves.

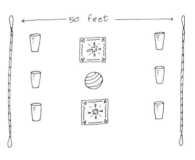

What to say
This game is called football because we'll only use our feet to play. I'll roll the playground ball down the centre of the playing area. Use your feet to roll and kick the ball to knock over

the cups on your opponents' side. If you use your hands, you must join the other group. Stay on your own side of the centre area! We'll play until one side has all their cups knocked down.

> **Inside tip**
> For older groups, dispense with the scarves and let players move over the entire field.

Crazy concentration

Get ready...

Group size: Eight or more
Best for ages: 5–7s
Playing time: Ten minutes
Energy level: Low
Items needed: Pairs of items such as two ping-pong balls, three pairs of cups, two rulers, two cotton headscarves, two balloons, or two skipping ropes

Get set...

Aim of the game
Give your memory a workout by matching pairs of items.

Go!

How to play
Invite each child to choose a game item from those you have set out. Then direct the children to sit in a circle and hide their items in their laps.

What to say

In many countries, children play games to strengthen their memories. Let's exercise our memories, too. We'll take turns finding pairs of items and placing them in the centre when a match is made. Choose a player to show his or her object and then point to the player you think is holding the matching object. If the guess is correct, the pair of items will be placed in the centre. If the guess is incorrect, both players will hide their items again and someone else has a turn.

The children whose items are matched may still point to players to find matching pairs. Continue playing until all the matching items are in the centre. Have children play once more but let them choose new items to match.

Inside tip

For a great memory-match warm-up, line up five or six items and let children look at them for a few seconds. Then hide the items and ask the children to recall what objects were shown and their order in the line.

 # Fast-food frenzy

Get ready...

Group size: Six or more
Best for ages: 5–11s
Playing time: Ten minutes
Energy level: High
Items needed: Two rulers and two skipping ropes

Get set...

Aim of the game

Be fast food and get bagged—not tagged!

Go!

How to play

Establish a starting line by laying both rulers at one end of the playing area. Make two skipping rope circles about 20 feet from the starting line. Tell the children that the circles are the fast-food 'bags'. Let the children decide which of the following fast-food items they'll be:

❖ Hamburgers   ❖ Chips   ❖ Pizzas   ❖ Sausages

Choose one person to be the caller. Then instruct all the fast food to stand behind the starting line.

What to say

This is a game of really fast food! The caller will name one or two fast-food items. The players who chose those food items will run to stand in the bags (skipping rope circles) before the caller tags them. In other words, you want to get bagged before you're tagged! Anyone who's tagged helps the caller tag more fast-food items.

Continue playing until all the food items have been tagged. The last player tagged becomes the next caller..

Inside tip

Let older children really whoop it up by allowing them to call as many fast-food items as they want and using only one bag. You may want to vary the mode of travel, such as hopping, walking backward or crawling to the bags. Make sure the caller moves in the same way as the 'food'.

Monkey maze

Get ready...

Group size: Eight or more
Best for ages: 5–7s
Playing time: 15 minutes
Energy level: Medium
Items needed: The kitchen timer and one game item for each player

Get set...

Aim of the game

Work your way through a crazy maze of monkeys before time runs out.

Go!

How to play

Set out the game items and invite each player to choose one. Tell the children that these items are pretend bananas. Set the kitchen timer at one end of the playing area. Choose two children to be the zoo keepers and have them set their 'bananas' at the opposite end of the playing area from the timer.

What to say

The zoo keepers are in a cage full of playful 'monkeys'. When I say 'monkey madness', the monkeys will create an obstacle course by touching their game items together. Monkeys can sit or stand or lie down or stretch their arms out or whatever. The monkeys must freeze in place that way. I'll start the timer and say 'go'. Then the zoo keepers must make their way through the maze of monkeys by crawling under the monkeys' arms or stepping over the monkeys to collect their own bananas before time runs out. When time's up, the monkeys can throw their bananas in the air and yell 'EEEK!'

Set the timer for one minute or less. Have the monkeys encourage the zoo keepers by squeaking 'eek, eek' as the zoo keepers pass. At the end of the first round, choose two new zoo keepers. You may wish to subtract five seconds for each round that the zoo keepers make it through the maze in time.

Inside tip
Young children really go 'ape' for this game. Play monkey maze to enrich your lessons on Noah's ark.

 # Hop 'n' pop

Get ready...

Group size: Any
Best for ages: 7–11s
Playing time: Ten minutes
Energy level: High
Items needed: The balloons and the masking tape

Get set...

Aim of the game
Keep hoppin' to save your balloon from poppin'.

How to play

Hand each child a balloon to blow up and tie off. Offer help to children who may not be able to tie their own balloons.
Hand everyone a ten-inch piece of masking tape. Direct children to tape one end of the masking tape to the knot on the balloon and the other end to their shoelace or shoe. Fold the tape in half between the shoe and balloon so that the tape sticks together.

What to say

We're going to get things hopping with this game. When I clap my hands, start hoppin' and poppin' balloons by stepping on them—but don't let your own balloon pop! If your balloon pops, sit down and help cheer the rest of the players on.

Continue until one player's balloon is left unpopped. That player may line up first for drinks or hand out more balloons and masking tape for another round.

Rock 'n' roll relay

Get ready...

Group size: Six or more
Best for ages: 9–11s
Playing time: 15 minutes
Energy level: High
Items needed: Two skipping ropes, two cotton headscarves, and two ping-pong balls

Get set...

Aim of the game
Help your group roll to the finish line first.

Go!

How to play
Establish a starting line by laying the skipping ropes at one end of the playing area. Lay the headscarves at the opposite end as a finish line. Have the children form two groups of 'rollers'. Show the rollers how to line up side by side on their hands and knees. Hand the last player in each line a ping-pong ball.

What to say
Let's get this game rolling, shall we? When I say 'rock 'n' roll', the last person in each line will lie on his or her side and roll across the backs of the rollers. When you get to the front of the line, roll the ping-pong ball underneath the rollers to the last person. Then that player will get rolling. Keep rockin' and rollin' until your group crosses the finish line.

Play the game again but this time have the players crawl under the rollers, instead of rolling across their backs.

 **Pat the cat**

Get ready...

Group size: Any
Best for ages: 5–7s
Playing time: 15 minutes
Energy level: Low
Items needed: Two cotton headscarves and a skipping rope

Get set...

Aim of the game
Pat the cat without getting caught.

Go!

How to play
Place a chair in front of the group. Choose one player to be the 'cat' and sit in the chair. Blindfold the cat with one headscarf and then place the other headscarf on the cat's head. Direct the other players to sit a few feet in front of the cat. Place the skipping rope in a circle a few feet away from the cat as the 'mouse hole'.

What to say
It's fun to pat a cat, but in this game you have to be fast, too. I'll secretly point to someone to sneak up and pat the cat by snatching the headscarf. If you're tagged by the cat, you turn into a mouse and must sit in the mouse hole. If you snatch the headscarf, you become the next cat.

Play until everyone has had a chance to be the cat.

45

Cool pass-offs

Get ready...

Group size: Any
Best for ages: 5–11s
Playing time: 10–15 minutes
Energy level: Medium
Items needed: The balloons and some water

Get set...

Aim of the game

Keep your balloon from popping as you cool off with watery fun.

Go!

How to play

This game is best played on a hot summer day. Make sure the children are wearing swimsuits or other clothes that can get wet.

Fill two balloons with water for each child. Form pairs and instruct them to line up facing each other, a foot apart. Hand each partner on one side of the line a water balloon and then set the rest of the water balloons aside.

What to say

When I clap my hands, throw the balloons to your partners. If the balloons are caught without popping, both partners take one step backward. Then I'll clap again, and you can throw your balloons back. We'll see who can keep catching their balloons the longest.

After one round, play another 'cool' game with the remainder of the water balloons. Have children stand in a circle.

What to say

When I say 'green light', begin passing two water balloons in opposite directions. When I say 'red light', stop passing the balloons. Whoever has a balloon must sit on the balloon and pop it. Then those people must sit in the centre of the circle.

Let the children begin passing two more balloons. Continue until all the water balloons have been popped.

Dodge-podge

Get ready...

Group size: Nine or more
Best for ages: 8–11s
Playing time: 15 minutes
Energy level: High
Items needed: The masking tape and the playground ball

Get set...

Aim of the game

Play cooperatively and tag opponents to join your group.

Go!

How to play

Establish a centre line by placing a strip of masking tape down the middle of the playing area. (If you're playing outside, use the skipping ropes for a centre line.) Form two groups on either side of the centre line and ask each group to number off by threes. Assign the following roles for each number:

❖ Ones can only catch the ball
❖ Twos can only throw the ball
❖ Threes can only pick up the ball

What to say

This game is played just like dodge ball, except you'll have to work together to tag your opponents with the ball. Each member of your group can only do what his or her number allows. If you're a one, you may only catch the ball; if you're a two, you may only throw the ball; and if you're a three, you may only pick up the ball. If you're tagged, you must join the other group.

Let the children continue playing until there is only one person left on a side. Remind children of their roles often until they get the hang of the game. Play the game again but re-number the children to play new roles.

Puppy-dog tails

Get ready...

Group size: Six or more
Best for ages: 5–9s
Playing time: 15 minutes
Energy level: High
Items needed: Two cotton headscarves

Get set...

Aim of the game
Be the first puppy to chase and snatch its opponents' tail.

Go!

How to play
Form two groups, or 'puppies', each group standing in a line. The first person in each line is the 'head' of the puppy. Have each child hold the waist of the person in front. Hand the last person in each puppy line a headscarf to tuck into his or her waistband or belt so that it hangs down like a tail. (For children who are not wearing a belt or don't have a waistband, let them hold the headscarf behind them like a tail.)

What to say
I can see you're puppies that are ready to play! When I say 'Chase 'em!' the head of each puppy will lead you in a chase to try to snatch the other puppy's tail. Don't let go of the person in front of you or your puppy is out!

Have the children play until the 'tail' of one puppy is snatched; then form new puppies and play again.

 **True or false**

Get ready...

Group size: Any
Best for ages: 6–11s
Playing time: Ten minutes
Energy level: Medium
Items needed: Two skipping ropes and a cotton headscarf

Get set...

Aim of the game

Help your group chase and capture your opponents before they reach their safety zone.

Go!

How to play

Lay the skipping ropes 30 feet apart, outside or in a large hall. Tell children that the areas behind the skipping ropes are the safety zones. Set the headscarf between the skipping ropes. Form two groups: the 'true' group and the 'false' group. Have groups line up facing each other on opposite sides of the headscarf.

What to say

We're going to play a great chase game of true and false. I'll tell you a sentence. If it's true, the true group chases the false group to their safety zone. But if the sentence is false, the false group chases the true group to their safety zone. Once in your safety zone, you can't be tagged. But if you're tagged while running, you must join the other group.

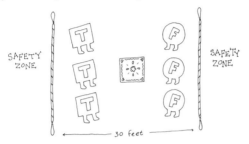

Use the following sentences, then make up more of your own. Let children take turns calling out true and false sentences.

❖ The sky is purple. (False)
❖ All children love to eat spinach. (False)
❖ Fish live under water. (True)
❖ There are 60 seconds in one minute. (True)
❖ Six plus three, take away two equals five. (False)

Play for ten minutes or until there are only a few children on one side.

Inside tip

This is a wonderful game to use when reviewing or reinforcing Bible stories and characters. Use statements such as 'Moses marched around the walls of Jericho' or 'Mary and Joseph took baby Jesus to Egypt'.

Moon balloon

Get ready...

Group size: Any
Best for ages: 6–11s
Playing time: 15 minutes
Energy level: Medium
Items needed: A skipping rope and the balloons

Get set...

Aim of the game

Help your group of astronauts be the first on the moon using rocket-ship balloons.

Go!

How to play

Place the skipping rope in a circle at one end of the playing area as the 'moon'. Form two groups of 'astronauts' and have them line up at the opposite end of the room from the moon. Hand each astronaut a balloon.

What to say

Each astronaut is holding a balloon rocket ship. When I say 'blast off!' the first astronaut will blow up his or her rocket ship, then let it go. The next astronaut in the group will run to the place where the rocket ship landed, blow up his or her balloon rocket ship and let it go. Continue taking turns launching your rocket ships until you make it to the moon.

Rocket ships don't need to land directly inside the circle moon but must be even with or travel beyond the moon for a successful moon landing!

 # Sneak peek

Get ready...

Group size: Any
Best for ages: 5–9s
Playing time: 15 minutes
Energy level: Medium
Items needed: A skipping rope, a cotton headscarf, and the kitchen timer

Get set...

Aim of the game

Sneak your way forward and be the first to snatch the headscarf.

Go!

How to play

Place the skipping rope at one end of the playing area as the starting line. Set the cotton headscarf at the opposite end. Choose one child to be the 'sneaky peeker' and have him or her stand behind the cotton headscarf. Have other children line up on the skipping rope.

What to say

Are you as quiet as a mouse? As fast as a rabbit? As sneaky as a fox? You'll need to be in this game! I'll start the timer. When the sneaky peeker turns his or her back and says 'sneak!' begin inching your way toward the headscarf. But when the sneaky peeker says 'peek!' freeze in place, or you'll have to go back to the starting line and begin again. The first one to sneak up and snatch the headscarf before time runs out becomes the next sneaky peeker.

Crocodile crawl

Get ready...

Group size: Six or more
Best for ages: 5–8s
Playing time: Ten minutes
Energy level: Medium
Items needed: Two skipping ropes, two cotton headscarves, six cups and six discs

Get set...

Aim of the game
Be part of a creepy crawly crocodile and collect items on your way to the swamp.

Go!

How to play
Establish start and finish lines at opposite ends of the playing area, using the skipping ropes and headscarves. Scatter six cups and six discs between the start and finish lines. Instruct children to form three groups or 'crocodiles' and line up single file behind the starting line. Tell children that the first person in each line is the

squat and hold the shoulders of

What to say

Look at the crawly crocodiles here today! I know you miss your swamp and want to go there for a swim. When I say 'go', begin creeping your way to the finish-line swamp, but along the way your crocodile must pick up two cups and two discs. Any part of the crocodile may pick up these items, not just the head. When you've collected your items, crawl to the swamp and roll over on your backs for a crocodile tickle.

Begin the game, then tickle the tummies of each crocodile that crosses the finish line. Form new crocodiles and play again.

Scoot for the loot

Get ready...

Group size: Eight or more
Best for ages: 5–11s
Playing time: 15 minutes
Energy level: Medium
Items needed: The masking tape, a cotton headscarf, and the colour and number cubes

Get set...

Aim of the game

Remember your secret colour and number, then be the first to grab the 'loot'.

Go!

How to play

Make a five-foot masking tape square on the floor and place the headscarf in the centre of it. Secretly assign each child a colour (red, yellow, green or blue) and a number from one to four. Tell the children they'll need to remember both their colour and their number. Invite the children to sit around the masking tape square.

What to say

Everyone knows how to scoot. Let's try it once. Scoot to the centre of the square. Pause as children scoot on their bottoms to the centre and back. In this game, you'll scoot for the 'loot' or the headscarf in the centre of the square. I'll roll the colour and number cubes and call out the colour and number rolled. Anyone with that colour and number must scoot to the centre of the square and be the first to grab the loot. Then that player becomes the next roller.

Play until everyone has had a chance to be the roller.

Inside tip

For an extra challenge with older children, make the square larger and have them scoot without using their hands.

Over, under, sideways, down

Get ready...

Group size: Six or more
Best for ages: 7–11s
Playing time: 15 minutes
Energy level: High
Items needed: The foam or playground ball, a disc, a skipping
                rope and the kitchen timer

Get set...

Aim of the game
Work together to beat the clock in this wacky passing game.

Go!

How to play
Have the children stand single file. Set the kitchen timer where
everyone can see it, such as on a chair or a table.

What to say
We'll try to beat the clock in this game by passing three
items in three different ways. We'll pass the ball over our heads,
the disc under our knees and the skipping rope sideways around
our waists. When the last person in the line receives an item,
they can set the item down. When all the items have been
passed, sit down quickly.

Start the timer. Continue until everyone is sitting down, and then
stop the timer. On the next round, ask the children to scramble
the order in which they are standing and try for a faster time.

Stepping stones

Get ready...

Group size: Any
Best for ages: 5–9s
Playing time: Ten minutes
Energy level: Medium
Items needed: Two skipping ropes, three cups and six discs

Get set...

Aim of the game
Help your partner walk on stepping stones to the finish line.

Go!

How to play
Establish start and finish lines at opposite ends of the playing area, using the skipping ropes. Set the cups behind the finish line.

Direct the children to find partners. (If there is an uneven number of children, someone can go twice or you may be someone's partner.) Have partners stand behind the starting line. Hand each pair two discs. Let partners decide who will be the 'stepper' and who will be the 'stone layer'.

What to say

Stepping stones help you get safely from one place to the next. In this game, the steppers cannot touch the ground but must walk on the stepping stones, or discs, that the stone layer sets down. You'll walk on the stepping stones to the finish line, pick up a cup, then swap places for the return trip to the starting line. The next pair will take the cup to the finish line and set it down. Let's practise stepping on the stones.

Demonstrate how to set down a disc and then have the stepper stand on that disc as you set down another. When the stepper lifts his or her first foot, pick up the disc and set it down again. Give children a few moments to practise, then begin the game. Continue playing until all the partners have had a chance to be steppers and stone layers.

> **Inside tip**
>
> This is a good game to reinforce the concept of following Jesus and letting him guide our steps in life.

Atoms and molecules

Get ready...

Group size: Six or more
Best for ages: 5–11s
Playing time: 15 minutes
Energy level: Medium
Items needed: Six discs and the kitchen timer

Get set...

Aim of the game

Travel in your 'molecule' and collect the most discs before time runs out.

Go!

How to play

Scatter the six discs around the playing area. Have children form groups of three to five 'molecules'. Direct the molecules to hold hands and form circles. Then have each molecule choose an 'atom' to stand in the centre.

What to say

Let's get a little atomic power moving today! You're all groups of molecules and have atoms standing in your centres.

The molecule's job is to protect its atom from being tagged by another molecule while it travels the playing field in search of power discs to pick up. The atom is the only part of your molecule allowed to pick up power discs. I'll start the timer, and you'll have one minute to pick up as many power discs as you can. If your atom is tagged by another molecule, your entire molecule must sit down.

Start the timer and after one minute call 'stop'. The molecule with the most discs gets to scatter the discs for the second round.

Inside tip
For an extra challenge, have members of each molecule stand with their backs facing inward and arms locked.

 Bouncing baubles

Get ready...

Group size: Eight or more
Best for ages: 5–11s
Playing time: 15 minutes
Energy level: Medium
Items needed: Two cotton headscarves, six discs, six cups, two ping-pong balls and the colour and number cubes

Get set...

Aim of the game
Form an assembly line and vault your pile of 'baubles' from one end to the other.

Go!

How to play

Form two groups and hand each group a headscarf, three discs, three cups, a ping-pong ball and a cube. Tell each group to choose a thrower and a catcher and then form a line. Instruct the thrower to stand a foot from the end of the line and the catcher a foot in front of the line. Have the children in between hold the edges of the headscarf. Place the rest of the 'baubles' beside the thrower.

What to say

You have a lot of pretty baubles that must go from the end of your line to the front, and you all have an important role in getting them there! When I say 'go', the thrower will throw a bauble to the players holding the headscarf. Those players will bounce the bauble on the headscarf and send it to the catcher, who catches the bauble and sets it down. We'll see which group is the fastest bauble bouncer!

Repeat the game a few times, mixing up the players each round. Try having throwers throw two baubles at once or begin passing a second bauble before the first is 'home'.

Whiplash

Get ready...

Group size: Any
Best for ages: 8–11s
Playing time: 15 minutes
Energy level: High
Items needed: Two discs, two skipping ropes and two cotton headscarves

Get set...

Aim of the game

Run to collect your group members and then whip to the disc and snatch it up!

Go!

How to play

Place two discs in the centre of the playing area. Form two groups. Hand one person a skipping rope and one person a headscarf in each group.

What to say

A whiplash moves back and forth very quickly. You're going to become a whiplash in a moment. The players with the skipping ropes will say, 'One, two, hip, hop, three, four, now stop!' You'll run and scatter until they say 'stop!' Then freeze in place. The players with the skipping ropes will run to gather their groups. The first player 'collected' in each group will hold on to the end of the skipping rope. Then the next player will hold on to the hand of the last player collected. When your whole group is together, run to the discs, but only the player holding the headscarf may pick up a disc.

Play until one group has picked up a disc; then form new groups and play again.

Inside tip

For extra excitement with older children, use only one disc. Or play the game without discs and create a jumbo whip to race around the playing area.

Cross the sea

Get ready...

Group size: Any
Best for ages: 7–11s
Playing time: Ten minutes
Energy level: Medium
Items needed: The skipping ropes and six discs

Get set...

Aim of the game
Throw the discs over the sea and then travel in odd ways to rescue them.

Go!

How to play
This game is best played outdoors. Lay the skipping ropes across the centre of the playing area as the 'sea'. Have the children stand 15 feet from the sea. Hand six children each a disc.

What to say
We'll all count one, two, three. On the count of three, the players with the discs will throw them across the sea like a frisbee. Then we'll say, 'Cross the sea and rescue me', and walk heel to toe to rescue the discs that flew out to sea. Whoever gets a disc will throw it next time.

If any discs fail to sail across the sea, don't rescue them until the other discs have been picked up. Play until everyone has had a turn to throw a disc. Vary the mode of travel, such as hopping, crawling, somersaulting or skipping to rescue the discs.

Gift giver

Get ready...

Group size: Any
Best for ages: 5–8s
Playing time: Ten minutes
Energy level: Low
Items needed: Six discs

Get set...

Aim of the game

Guess who gave you a 'gift' and be the next 'giver'.

Go!

How to play

Gather the children in a group on the floor. Hand six children each a disc. If your group is small, use only two or three discs.

What to say

I've just handed pretend gifts to six 'givers'. In a moment you'll hide your eyes and put one of your hands in the air. The givers will sneak around the room and each place a gift in someone's hand. When we say, 'Five, four, three, two, guess who gave a gift to you!' open your eyes. Then you'll have one try to guess who gave you the gift. If you're right, you're the next giver.

Play until everyone's had a chance to be a giver.

Inside tip

Play this game at the start of the year. It's a great icebreaker and helps everyone learn new names.

Upside-downside

Get ready...

Group size: Any
Best for ages: 5–9s
Playing time: Ten minutes
Energy level: High
Items needed: Two rulers and six cups

Get set...

Aim of the game

Take turns racing to turn your cups upside down and then right side up.

Go!

How to play

Lay the rulers at one end of the playing area as two starting lines. Place three cups in a row, beginning five feet from each starting line. Make sure there are five feet between the cups in each row. Form two groups and let players huddle to decide how they'll travel. For example, they may choose to run, walk heel to toe, crawl, or hop on one foot. Tell them that each person in their group must choose a different way to travel. Then have players line up single file behind their starting lines.

What to say

    In this game you'll travel in your special way to the cups. The first players will turn their three cups upside down. Then they'll run back and sit down. The next players will travel in their special ways and set the cups right side up. We'll continue until everyone is sitting down.

Begin the relay by saying 'go'. The first group sitting down gets to line up first for refreshments.

Human jacks

Get ready...

Group size: Six or more
Best for ages: 5–8s
Playing time: 15 minutes
Energy level: High
Items needed: The playground ball

Get set...

Aim of the game

Play a giant game of jacks and make number groups.

Go!

How to play

Stand in a circle. Choose one child to be the thrower and hand him or her the playground ball.

What to say

This game is played like jacks, only we're using people instead of jacks. The thrower will throw the ball high in the air and begin by calling out 'onesies'. You must form groups of one before the thrower catches the ball. Then the thrower will throw the ball again and say 'twosies'. Run to form groups of two before he or she catches the ball. If you can't find a group before the thrower catches the ball, sit down until he or she calls the next group number. We'll continue until everyone forms one large group.

Continue playing until each child has been the thrower.

Inside tip

This game is also fun when you use items from the game bag. Set a variety of items near the thrower and, when a number is called, have the children run to assemble the number of items called.

Swirlin' Sam

Get ready...

Group size: Any
Best for ages: 5–7s
Playing time: Ten minutes
Energy level: High
Items needed: Two skipping ropes

Get set...

Aim of the game

Jump over the swirling ropes and sing your favourite songs.

Go!

How to play

Tie the skipping ropes together to make one long rope. Choose someone to be Swirlin' Sam and hand him or her the skipping rope.

What to say

Swirlin' Sam is going to get things jumping! Sam will twirl the skipping rope around in a low circle while we jump over the rope. As we jump, we'll repeat a counting verse. Then we'll see how many jumps we can make before someone misses. When someone misses, we'll choose a new Swirlin' Sam.

Repeat the following rhyme as children jump over the rope. When someone misses, choose a new Swirlin' Sam and begin again. Use other skipping rope chants or sing songs as children jump.

Blue-berry, straw-berry, huckle-berry-boo.
How many jumps can we do?
(Begin counting jumps)

Inside tip

Children love to skip! Leave the ropes tied together and jump in the traditional way with two children twirling the rope. Use the same rhyme and let the children try to better their own 'jumping score' with each turn.

 Frogs on the lily pads

Get ready...

Group size: Any
Best for ages: 5–8s
Playing time: Ten minutes
Energy level: High
Items needed: Six discs and the colour and number cubes

Get set...

Aim of the game
Be leaping frogs and capture a lily pad.

Go!

How to play
Place the discs at one end of the playing area as 'lily pads'. Gather the children at the opposite end and have them team up with a friend. Assign each pair a colour (red, yellow, green or blue).

What to say

You're frogs hopping to lily pads. I'll roll the colour and number cubes. If your colour is rolled, you and your froggy partner will leapfrog the number of times rolled on the number cube. For example, if I roll yellow and the number three, the yellow frog pairs will leapfrog three times toward the lily pads. When you reach a lily pad, sit on it. We'll play until all the lily pads are captured.

If your group is smaller than twelve, use fewer lily pads. You may also play this game with individual hopping frogs.

Fore by four

Get ready...

Group size: Up to 12
Best for ages: 9–11s
Playing time: 15 minutes
Energy level: Medium
Items needed: Six cups and two ping-pong balls

Get set...

Aim of the game

Play a round of goofy golf and be the foursome with the least number of strokes.

Go!

How to play

Put six cups on their sides around the playing area. Invite the children to form foursomes and choose one person to be the driver, one to be the putter, and two children to be the hitters. (If you have a small group, partners can double up by being a driver/hitter and a putter/hitter. If your group is larger than eight, have extra children to be hitters.) Hand each group a ping-pong ball. Gather children at one end of the playing area.

What to say

It's a great day for a game of goofy golf. There are six cups or 'holes' in our goofy golf course. You'll play each hole and work in your groups to get the lowest score. The drivers kick the ping-pong balls first each time and aim toward any cup. Then the hitters each take a turn kicking the ball closer to the cup. Finally, the putters can gently tap the ball into the cup with their feet. No hands allowed in this game! Then begin again and aim toward another cup. Keep track of your kicks or 'strokes'. Then we'll see who has the lowest number at the end of six holes.

When everyone has finished the course, let the group with the lowest score hand out special 19th-hole treats such as marshmallow 'golf balls' or Polo 'holes'.

 **Freeze ball**

Get ready...

Group size: Any
Best for ages: 5–11s
Playing time: 15 minutes
Energy level: High
Item needed: The playground ball

Get set...

Aim of the game
Don't get tagged by the ball while you're frozen in place.

Go!

How to play
This game is best when played outdoors or in a large hall. Have the children stand in the centre of the playing area. Hand one player the playground ball and designate this player as 'Frosty'.

What to say
In this game, Frosty will try to turn you into freezing ice cubes. When Frosty throws the ball in the air, run and scatter. But when Frosty catches the ball and shouts 'Freeze!' you must stop. Then Frosty will take three giant steps toward any player and throw the ball at waist level or below. You may stoop or swivel to dodge the ball, but one foot must remain frozen in place. If you catch the ball, you become the next Frosty. If you're tagged, you become an ice cube and must sit down. We'll play until there's only one person who's not an ice cube.

Switch-o, change-o

Get ready...

Group size: At least seven
Best for ages: 5–11s
Playing time: Ten minutes
Energy level: High
Items needed: The colour cube

Get set...

Aim of the game

Hurry to switch places but don't get caught without a spot!

Go!

How to play

Sit the children in a large circle and assign each player a colour (red, yellow, green or blue). Instruct the children to remember their colours. Choose someone to be 'it' and squat in the centre of the circle holding the colour cube.

What to say

You've got to be a quick-change artist in this game. The person who is 'it' will roll the colour cube and call out the colour rolled. All the players with that colour must stand up and hop to change places with someone else of that colour. The person who is 'it' will try to get into one of the empty spots, too, so you'll have to switch-o, change-o quickly! The player caught without a place becomes the next 'it'.

Vary the way children change places, such as skipping, inching on their bottoms, or walking backwards. Continue playing until each person has had a turn at being 'it' and rolling the colour cube.

> ### Inside tip
> Older children enjoy spreading out rather than playing in a circle. Let older children run to change places but tell them to be careful of collisions.

Kangaroo hop

Get ready...

Group size: Any
Best for ages: 5–7s
Playing time: Ten minutes
Energy level: High
Items needed: Two skipping ropes, two cotton headscarves, the playground ball and the foam ball

Get set...

Aim of the game
Be the first group of hopping kangaroos to travel to the zoo and back.

Go!

How to play
Establish start and finish lines by laying the skipping ropes 20 feet apart or at opposite ends of the playing area. Place the two headscarves behind the finish line. Have the children form two groups of 'kangaroos' and direct them to stand in single file lines behind the starting line. Hand the first kangaroo in each group a ball.

What to say
I can see lots of kangaroos ready for a good hop. When I say 'go', the first kangaroos will place the balls between their knees, hop to the zoo or finish line, and pick up the scarves. Then hop back to your group and hand the ball and the scarf to the next kangaroo. We'll keep things hopping until all the kangaroos have gone to the zoo and back.

Satellite spin

Get ready...

Group size: Any
Best for ages: 5–11s
Playing time: Ten minutes
Energy level: Medium
Item needed: A disc

Get set...

Aim of the game
Keep the satellite in orbit by continually spinning it.

Go!

How to play

Have the children sit in a circle and number off so that each child has a different number. (If your group is very large, form two circles and use two discs to play.) Remind the children what the number span is (such as one to eight or one to 14, depending on the size of your group). Instruct them to remember their own number.

What to say

This disc is a satellite and our mission is to keep it in orbit. I'll launch the satellite by giving it a spin. Then I'll call out a number from one to [whatever your span is]. The player with that number must run to the centre and give the satellite another spin before it stops. Then he or she can call out another number. We'll see how long we can keep the satellite in orbit.

Be sure everyone has a chance to spin the satellite at least once. For an extra challenge with older groups, use multiple discs and keep them all spinning.

Fireflies and firefighters

Get ready...

Group size: Up to 20
Best for ages: 5–11s
Playing time: 15 minutes
Energy level: High
Item needed: Six cups, the kitchen timer and some water

Get set...

Aim of the game
Tag the fireflies before time runs out and their fires are quenched.

Go!

How to play
This is a summer game and should be played outside when the children are dressed in swimsuits or old clothes. Fill six cups with water. Form two groups and designate one group as the taggers. Instruct the other group to form pairs and choose which partners will be the fireflies and which will be the firefighters. Hand each firefighter a cup of water.

What to say
This is a hot game! I'll turn over the timer and say 'fire!' The taggers will run to tag fireflies. If any fireflies are tagged, they must sit down until a firefighter pours water on them. The firefly is then free to fly again. If a firefighter runs out of water, he or she must sit down. Taggers will try to capture all the fireflies before time runs out or the water runs dry.

After you've played, refill the cups and play again. Play until everyone has been a firefly.

Inside tip
This is a great game to play at a picnic gathering, where most adults will love to join in the action.

Zigzag-zally

Get ready...

Group size: Ten or more
Best for ages: 8–11s
Playing time: Ten minutes
Energy level: Low
Items needed: The playground ball and the foam ball

Get set...

Aim of the game
Be the first group to throw your ball zigzag up and down the line.

Go!

How to play
Have the children number off by twos. Direct the two groups to stand in two lines, about three feet apart, each player facing a member of the other group. Hand a ball to the player standing at the end of each line.

What to say
This is a zany zigzag game. You'll be throwing the balls in zigzag fashion to your group members. When I say 'go', the first person in each line will

throw the ball to the group member diagonally opposite him or her. The first players catching the balls will say 'zig', and then the second players will say 'zag', and the next will say 'zally', and so on down the line. Then throw the ball back up the line. The group who zigzag-zallies up and down the line first chooses the next game.

> ## Inside tip
> For older children, decide on how many zigzag-zallies must be completed for a game. Try using balloons for a different twist.

 # Crazy crickets

Get ready...

Group size: Any
Best for ages: 5–11s
Playing time: 15 minutes
Energy level: Medium
Items needed: The masking tape and the playground ball

Get set...

Aim of the game
Jump over the ball before you get tagged.

Go!

How to play
Use the masking tape to make a ten-foot-diameter circle on the floor. Then divide the circle into four equal sections with masking tape lines.

Choose two children to be rollers and have them stand on opposite sides of the circle. Hand one of the rollers the playground ball. Direct the rest of the children, or 'crickets', to stand in the quarter sections of the circle. Tell them they must remain in those sections for the entire game.

What to say
Crickets are high jumpers, especially in this game. The rollers will roll the ball back and forth across the circle. Jump over the ball before it tags you. If you're tagged, you become a roller and help tag other crickets. Remember, you must stay in your section of the circle! We'll play until there's only one cricket left.

Inside tip

Older children enjoy this game as much as younger ones. Add an extra challenge by playing with two balls and let the crickets roam the entire circle to dodge the balls.

Whale tail

Get ready...

Group size: Any
Best for ages: 5–7s
Playing time: 15 minutes
Energy level: Low
Items needed: A cotton headscarf

Get set...

Aim of the game
Don't get caught snatching the whale's tail.

Go!

How to play

Choose a child to be the 'whale' and sit with his or her back to the group. Lay the headscarf behind the whale.

What to say

We can be secret whale-tail snatchers. I'll point to someone to sneak up and silently snatch the whale's tail. When he or she returns, we'll all hide our hands in our laps. We'll try to fool the whale so he or she won't know who has the tail. Then we'll say, 'Whopping whale, who has your tail?' The whale will have two chances to find the missing tail. If the whale guesses correctly, the snatcher becomes the next whale. If the whale doesn't find the tail, we'll play again, and the person who had the tail may point to the next tail snatcher.

Continue playing until each child has snatched the tail at least once.

Inside tip

If you have a large group of children, play a variation called Fish Fins. Use two scarves as fins and have two snatchers.

Hurricane

Get ready...

Group size: Any
Best for ages: 5–11s
Playing time: 15 minutes
Energy level: Medium
Items needed: The masking tape and the balloons

Get set...

Aim of the game
Huff 'n' puff 'n' blow the balloon to another group before it touches the floor.

Go!

How to play
Make a five-foot-diameter circle on the floor with masking tape. Then divide the circle into thirds with masking tape lines. Have the children number off by threes. Direct each group to stand in one section of the circle with their hands behind their backs. Inform the children that they'll remain in these sections for the entire game. To promote team spirit, encourage each group to create a name for themselves, such as the Silver Streaks or the Jumping Jacks. Blow up and tie off a few balloons and then set them aside.

What to say
Hurricanes really blow, and that's what we'll do in this game. I'll throw a balloon into the centre of the circle. You'll work with your groups to blow the balloon to someone else's area of the circle. Don't let the balloon touch the floor in your section. And no hands allowed—just lots of huffs 'n' puffs!

Play until the balloon touches the floor. Then play again using two balloons. End the game by keeping three balloons in play. You may wish to add an extra challenge by asking the players to kneel.

 Steal the deal

Get ready...

Group size: Any
Best for ages: 5–7s
Playing time: 15 minutes
Energy level: Low
Items needed: The colour cube, the playground ball, the kitchen timer, and one less item than there are children

Get set...

Aim of the game
Be the player with the colour cube when time runs out.

Go!

How to play
Have the children sit in a circle with their legs crossed and their knees touching the people on either side to create a solid circle. Hand one child the colour cube and give the rest of the children each a game item. Tell them to set their items in front of them on the floor.

What to say
        In this game you'll try to bowl over items and take them. I'll set the timer and then we'll take turns rolling the ball around the circle. If you hit someone's item, he or she must give it to you

to set in front of you. You may even hit two or three things with one roll! When the time runs out, the person with the colour cube begins the next game.

 # Save the king or queen!

Get ready...

Group size: Ten or more
Best for ages: 8–11s
Playing time: 20 minutes
Energy level: High
Items needed: Two skipping ropes and two cotton headscarves

Get set...

Aim of the game
Free your group's king or queen and bring them safely over the centre line.

Go!

How to play
This game is best played outdoors or in a large hall. Lay the skipping ropes down the centre of the playing area. Place each headscarf 20 feet behind the centre line on each side. Designate one side of the centre line as a jail. Have children form two groups and stand on opposite sides of the centre line. Let each group choose a king or queen to be a prisoner and stand on the opponent's headscarf. Then let each group choose a guard to guard the opponents' 'royalty'. The rest of the players may run anywhere on their side of the centre line.

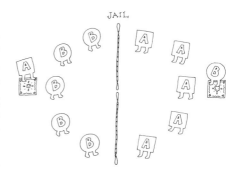

What to say

This is a royal rescue game! Your group will attempt to rescue your king or queen without getting tagged by the guard or your opponents. If you're tagged, go to jail until one of your team members runs to tag you free. Then the two of you may safely return to your side and resume playing. If you reach the king or queen without being tagged, you've won the game.

Inside tip

Older children love this fast-paced rescue game! Let the winning team line up first for much-needed refreshments after playing.

Mall-brawl

Get ready...

Group size: Any
Best for ages: 5–9s
Playing time: Ten minutes
Energy level: High
Items needed: A cotton headscarf and one less playing item
                    than there are children

Get set...

Aim of the game

Rush to exchange purchases with someone else—but don't get caught without a package!

Go!

How to play

Designate the 'store' by placing a headscarf on the floor in the centre of the playing area. Lay the playing items beside the store. Choose one player to be the mall-caller and then invite everyone else to choose a playing item from the store. Direct the children to spread out around the playing area.

What to say

Everyone rushes to shop and exchange items in a shopping mall. In this game you'll rush to exchange the item you have with the item someone else has. When the mall-caller says 'mall-brawl', quickly rush to set your items in the centre. Then choose a different item and return to your place. The mall-caller will also rush to pick up an item. The person left without a 'package' becomes the next mall-caller. You must pick up a different item each time.

> ### Inside tip
>
> Try this game with older children, too. They love the idea of shopping malls, and the game is a great icebreaker when they exchange packages (and names!) with each other.

Follow-the-leader toss-up

Get ready...

Group size: Any
Best for ages: 5–8s
Playing time: Ten minutes
Energy level: Medium
Items needed: The playground ball and one item for each player

Get set...

Aim of the game

Follow the leader's tricks and then challenge the others with your tricks.

Go!

How to play

Choose one player to be the leader and give him or her the playground ball. Invite the rest of the players each to choose a playing item. Form a circle with the leader in the centre.

What to say

The leader will throw the ball in the air and then do a trick such as clapping three times or twirling around before catching the ball. If the leader makes a successful catch, imitate his or her trick using your item. If the leader drops the ball, we'll choose another leader. After the leader has done three tricks, we'll pass our items five places to the right and then choose a new leader. Let's play until everyone has had a chance to lead.

Encourage the leaders to devise new, unique tricks. When a new leader steps to the centre, they should hand their item to the outgoing leader.

 # Bee-bop 'n' doo-wop

Get ready...

Group size: Any
Best for ages: 6–11s
Playing time: Ten minutes
Energy level: Medium
Items needed: The balloons

Get set...

Aim of the game
Have fun boppin' your balloons but be ready to switch directions in a wink.

Go!

How to play
Hand each player a balloon to blow up and tie off. Help younger children to blow up and tie off their balloons. Stand in a close-knit circle.

Sing in your own little tune: 'Bee-bop 'n' doo-wop. Bee-bee-bop 'n' doo-wop'.

What to say
Keep the 'bee-bop 'n' doo-wop' song going as you bop your balloons. We'll start by bopping our balloons up and down.

Then when I say 'bee-bop', bop your balloon to the player on your right. Keep bopping to the right until I say 'doo-wop', then reverse directions and bop your balloon to the player on your left. Keep bopping to the left and right depending on the call. When I finally say 'stop', we'll see if you have a balloon to hold.

Inside tip

Try a variation of this game. Bop one less balloon than there are children around the circle. When you say 'stop', the player without a balloon becomes the next 'bee-bop 'n' doo-wop' caller.

Alpha-pass

Get ready...

Group size: Any
Best for ages: 5–11s
Playing time: 15 minutes
Energy level: Low
Items needed: The foam ball and the kitchen timer

Get set...

Aim of the game

Pass your way through the alphabet before time runs out.

Go!

How to play

Form a circle. Hand one player the foam ball.

What to say

This is a game of fast catching and quick thinking. I'll name a category such as 'food' and then begin the timer. I'll name a food that begins with the letter 'a', such as artichoke. Then I'll quickly toss the ball to someone across the circle, who can name a food beginning with the letter 'b'. If someone tosses you the ball and you've already named a food, toss the ball quickly to someone who hasn't had a turn. After everyone's participated, we'll repeat turns. Let's see if we can make it through the alphabet before time runs out.

Play again using a category suggested below or make up more of your own. If you're playing with young children, omit the timer and let them simply repeat the alphabet letter by letter. Categories may include:

❖ Animals
❖ Cereal names
❖ Names of girls or boys

❖ Names of countries
❖ Objects in a classroom
❖ Articles of clothing

Stash-and-dash pirates

Get ready...

Group size: Any
Best for ages: 5–8s
Playing time: 15 minutes
Energy level: Medium
Items needed: The kitchen timer, six discs and six cups

Get set...

Aim of the game
Find all the hidden objects before time runs out.

Go!

How to play

Choose two children to be pirates and hand them the discs and the cups. The rest of the children will be dashers.

What to say

Pirates always stash their loot. In a moment the dashers will hide their eyes and count to 20 while the pirates hide their loot around the playing area. Then the pirates will call out 'stash and dash!' I'll begin the timer, and the dashers can run to find the hidden loot and bring it back to the timer. We'll play until the loot is found or time runs out.

Have the dashers turn with their backs to the pirates as they count to 20. Continue playing until each player has been a pirate and has had a chance to hide the loot.

Inside tip

The pirates can give clues to help the dashers, if they're having trouble finding the loot. Let the pirates clap more quickly, the closer the dashers get to finding the hidden loot.

 **Accelerate!**

Get ready...

Group size: Five or more
Best for ages: 6–9s
Playing time: Ten minutes
Energy level: Low
Item needed: The playground ball

Get set...

Aim of the game
Throw the ball faster and faster in a fixed pattern without dropping it.

Go!

How to play
Ask everyone to stand in a circle. If you have more than eight children, form two or three smaller circles. Hand one player the playground ball.

What to say
Let's have some fun making patterns. The first person will throw the ball to someone in the circle. Then that player will throw the ball to someone else

SAMPLE PATTERN FOR TOSSING

and so on. Each person should throw the ball to someone new until everyone in the circle has caught the ball once. Then we'll begin the pattern all over again. Remember who you threw the ball to! Keep throwing in your pattern until I say 'accelerate!' Then speed up your throwing until I say 'brakes' or someone drops the ball. Then we'll stop and begin a new pattern.

Wait until the children are familiar with the throwing pattern before calling out 'accelerate!' After a few rounds, try adding a second ball for really exciting play.

Inside tip
If you have a very large group, make a smaller circle and use any throwable playing item, such as the colour or number cubes or the cups.

Across the border

Get ready...

Group size: Nine or more
Best for ages: 8–11s
Playing time: 15 minutes
Energy level: High
Items needed: The masking tape, six cups and the kitchen timer

Get set...

Aim of the game

Have the least number of cups behind your goal line when time runs out.

Go!

How to play

Place three four-foot masking tape lines on the playing field. Place the lines in a triangle shape as shown, about 15 feet apart. Form three groups and have each group choose a 'goalie'. (If there are more than nine children in each group,

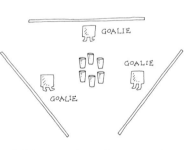

let each group choose two goalies.) Direct each goalie to stand in front of a masking tape line. Set the six cups in the centre. Tell the rest of the children to stand near the cups.

What to say

In this game you'll try to get cups over the other groups' goal lines. When I start the timer and say 'go', grab a cup and attempt to set it behind any opponent's goal line. The goalie's job is to quickly return the cups to the centre. You may only carry one cup at a time. We'll play until time runs out and I say 'freeze'. Then we'll count the cups behind each goal line.

Begin the game and play until time runs out. If you're using two goalies for each group, have the winning team cut back to one goalie for the next round.

 **Big boom**

Get ready...

Group size: Any
Best for ages: 5–7s
Playing time: 15 minutes
Energy level: Low
Item needed: The colour cube

Get set...

Aim of the game
Don't be caught with the dynamite in this exciting counting game.

Go!

How to play
Form a circle. Choose a player to be 'it'. Have that person choose a number between one and 25 and whisper it to you. This number is the 'big boom'.

What to say

This is an exciting game of counting. The person chosen to be 'it' chose a number between one and 25 and whispered that number to me. We'll begin passing the colour cube around the circle. As we pass it, we'll count, 'one, two, three, four, five' and so on until we get to the number that's the big boom. Then 'it' will shout 'Big boom!' and the player holding the colour cube comes to the centre and becomes the next person to be 'it'.

Continue playing until each player has been 'it'. You may want to play the game like musical chairs and have the children sit in the centre of the circle after they've received a big boom. Play until one child remains in the circle, with the 'it' choosing a new number each time. Older children may enjoy using higher numbers that are multiples of five or ten, then counting in fives or tens to reach that number.

> **Inside tip**
>
> If your group is very large, pass two items and choose two 'big boom' numbers.

Put out the fire

Get ready...

Group size:	Any
Best for ages:	5–11s
Playing time:	15 minutes
Energy level:	High
Items needed:	Six cups and some water

Get set...

Aim of the game
Cool off with exciting water fun.

Go!

How to play
This game is best played outdoors on a hot summer day. Make sure children are in swimsuits or clothes that can get wet. Fill six cups with water and place them around the playing field. Gather the children at one end of the playing field.

What to say
It's a hot day, and you look like sizzling matches that need cooling off with a bit of water. When I say, 'put out the fire!' run to a cup and stick one of your fingers in the water. You may have up to four people at each cup. The next time I say, 'put out the fire', run to a different cup and stick two fingers in the water. If a cup tips over, the people at that cup must sit down for the remainder of the game. We'll play until we get to ten fingers or until all the cups are tipped over.

Refill the cups after the first round and let children play once more. Be sure to invite children to have cool drinks of water in paper cups when you're finished playing.

Power-partner polo

Get ready...

Group size: Eight or more
Best for ages: 7–11s
Playing time: 15 minutes
Energy level: High
Items needed: Two skipping ropes and six cups

Get set...

Aim of the game

Kick the cup across your opponent's goal line.

Go!

How to play

This game needs a large
playing area and is best suited
to be played out of doors or in
a large hall. Lay the skipping
ropes 50 feet apart as goal
lines and set six cups in the
centre of the playing area.
Have the children form two groups and stand on opposite sides of
the cups. Instruct the children to find partners and lock arms.

What to say

In this game of polo, partners will run and kick cups over
their opponents' goal line. Keep your arms locked—no hands are
allowed in this game. You may block your opponents' shots to
prevent them from kicking cups over your group's goal line, and
you may 'steal' the cup by kicking it away from your opponents.

When a cup goes over a goal line, leave it there until the end of the game. We'll play until all the cups are over the goal lines.

When all the cups are over the goal lines, count the number of cups on each side. The group with the fewest number may choose the next game.

 # Backpack pass

Get ready...

Group size: Any
Best for ages: 6–11s
Playing time: Ten minutes
Energy level: Medium
Items needed: The colour and number cubes

Get set...

Aim of the game
Wiggle and jiggle to pass the backpack down your line.

Go!

How to play
Form two groups and instruct each group to line up on their hands and knees beside each other. Place a cube on the back of the first person in each line.

What to say
I can see you're on pretend school buses, ready for school. But you forgot your backpacks! When I say 'go', pass your

'backpack' to the end of your bus. You'll have to really wiggle and jiggle to pass it back—no hands allowed! If the backpack falls off a player, that player goes to the back of the bus. Then the next person in line sets the backpack on his or her back and passes it on. The first group to pass the backpack to the end of the bus wins.

Inside tip

Let children pass the backpack in different ways, such as with their feet, their knees, or their elbows.

Lost sheep

Get ready...

Group size: Any
Best for ages: 5–8s
Playing time: 15 minutes
Energy level: Low
Items needed: The kitchen timer, two cotton headscarves and the number and colour cubes

Get set...

Aim of the game

Find the lost sheep before time runs out.

Go!

How to play

Have children form a circle sitting on the floor. Choose two children to be 'shepherds' and blindfold them. As you explain the game, wind up the timer and set it somewhere in the circle.

What to say
Our two shepherds have lost a sheep and must crawl on their hands and knees to find it. The timer will be our pretend sheep. If you're very quiet, you can hear the lost sheep. Listen for the tick of the timer. All right, shepherds, go and find your lost sheep.

Play until one of the shepherds has found the sheep. Then blindfold two more children and hide the timer. Play until each child has been a shepherd.

Inside tip

For a fun variation, or if you're using a timer that doesn't make ticking sounds, choose only one shepherd. Hide the colour cube and let the children in the circle clap faster as the shepherd moves closer to the sheep, and slower when he or she moves away.

 # Rahab rag-tag

Get ready...

Group size: Any
Best for ages: 5–11s
Playing time: 15 minutes
Energy level: High
Items needed: Two cotton headscarves

Get set...

Aim of the game
Grab Rahab's rope before you're tagged out.

Go!

How to play

This is a great game to reinforce your study of Joshua at Jericho. Gather children in the centre of the playing area. Choose the two children whose birthdays are closest to today's date to be 'Rahabs'. Hand the Rahabs the headscarves and tell them to place the scarves on their shoulders or heads.

What to say

Let's pretend the scarves in this game are Rahab's red rope. When I say, 'Rahab rag-tag', try to snatch the 'rope' from each Rahab without getting tagged. If either Rahab tags you, you must sit out for the remainder of the round. Whoever snatches a rope becomes Rahab in the next game.

Continue playing until each child has been a Rahab. Add an extra challenge for older players by choosing a partner to guard each Rahab from the rope snatchers. The guards may tag players instead of Rahab.

Inside tip

This game can easily be adapted for smaller playing spaces. Clear a space in your meeting venue and instruct children to walk heel to toe or backwards to play.

Guardian angels

Get ready...

Group size: Any
Best for ages: 5–11s
Playing time: 15 minutes
Energy level: High
Items needed: Six cups and the playground ball

Get set...

Aim of the game
Pretend to be angels and guard Daniel from the lion's jaws.

Go!

How to play
Hand a cup to each player and tell the children that these are 'Daniels'. If you have more than six players, let children play in pairs. (For really large groups, omit the cups and play with threesomes: two guardian angels and one child as Daniel.) Instruct the players to set their cups on the floor and stand beside them.

What to say
In this game you're all guardian angels, and you're guarding Daniel (your cup) from the jaws of a ferocious lion! This ball is our pretend lion. You'll roll the lion at each other's Daniel and try to knock it over. Guard Daniel by deflecting the lion with your feet. No hands are allowed in this game, so you'll have to

roll—not kick—the ball with your feet. We'll play until there's only one Daniel left standing.

Inside tip

Older children love this game as much as younger players. For a twist, have the children form a circle and place the cups inside the circle. Choose two or three 'guardian angels' and let children in the circle roll the lion quickly back and forth across the circle as the angels guard the cups from tipping over.

Step across the sea

Get ready...

Group size: Any
Best for ages: 5–7s
Playing time: Ten minutes
Energy level: Medium
Items needed: Six discs and two cotton headscarves

Get set...

Aim of the game
Don't fall in the sea as you step across the stones.

Go!

How to play
Lay the headscarves at opposite ends of the classroom or 20 feet apart in a larger play area. Place the discs at equal intervals between the scarves. Gather children behind one of the scarves.

What to say

What a big sea we must cross! And we can only step on the discs or 'stones' to cross it. We'll start at the headscarves and hop from stone to stone until we reach the other scarf. Each time we cross the sea without falling in, we'll spread the stones a little farther apart. Do you think we can cross the sea three or four or even five times?

Each time everyone makes it across the sea, move the discs a few more inches apart. You may even have to remove a disc if your group is full of leaps and bounds!

Balloon serenade

Get ready...

Group size: Any
Best for ages: 8–11s
Playing time: Ten minutes
Energy level: Low
Items needed: The balloons and a ruler

Get set...

Aim of the game
Outlast the entire orchestra with your balloon serenade.

Go!

How to play
This game is great fun but best played in an outside 'amphitheatre' where others won't be disturbed by the serenades. Hand each

player a balloon. Instruct children to blow up the balloons and hold the ends to prevent escaping air. As you explain the game, swing the ruler back and forth a few times like a conductor's baton.

What to say

You're part of the 'Squeak 'n' Squawk Balloon Orchestra'. I'll be your conductor. When I say 'begin', create your own serenade by letting squeaky sounds come from your balloon. Watch my baton as I conduct the orchestra! When I wave the baton faster, play faster. But if I slow down, you slow down, too. We'll play until the very last squeaky-squawking note. Whoever plays the last note of the serenade becomes the next conductor.

At the end of the serenade, hand the ruler to the next conductor and ask the children to blow up their balloons for the second overture. End your serenade with a bang by letting the children blow up their balloons, tie them, then sit on the balloons on the count of three.

Funny fishing

Get ready...

Group size: Any
Best for ages: 7–11s
Playing time: 15 minutes
Energy level: Low
Items needed: The masking tape, two skipping ropes, two ping-pong balls, six discs, six cups, and two cotton headscarves

Get set...

Aim of the game
Be the first group of fishers to pull in your catch.

Go!

How to play
Invite children to form two groups of 'fishers', and hand each group a skipping rope 'fishing pole'. Let groups each choose someone to be a 'fish', and have the fish stand three feet from their group. Place a ping-pong ball, a headscarf, three cups and three discs beside each fish. Set the masking tape between the fish.

What to say
It's a fine day to go fishing! The first fisher in each group will cast a line (skipping rope) to the fish. The fish must tear off a piece of masking tape and tape an item on the end of the line. Tug on the line, and the fisher can pull in the catch. Then the fisher runs to become the next fish, and the fish runs to join the group of fishers. We'll continue until all your items have been caught and reeled in.

If your group is large, have two players to be fish and let the fishers take turns casting the lines.

Galloping Goliaths

Get ready...

Group size: Any
Best for ages: 9–11s
Playing time: Ten minutes
Energy level: High
Items needed: Two skipping ropes, two cotton headscarves and six cups

Get set...

Aim of the game
Be the first group of galloping Goliaths through the obstacle course.

Go!

How to play
Place the skipping ropes at one end of the playing area and the headscarves at the opposite end to create two start and finish lines. Stagger the cups between the start and finish lines, making sure  there are at least three feet between each cup. Instruct children to form threesomes. Have the trios line up behind the starting lines.

What to say
The Bible tells us that Goliath was giant-sized, maybe even as big as three children! Your threesomes are 'Goliaths' in this race. When I say 'go', two players in each trio will cross arms and grasp each other's wrists. The third person will sit on their arms.

Walk and weave around the three cups until you reach the finish line. Then your trio can grab hands and run back to the starting line. When all the Goliaths in your group have finished, sit down and shout 'Go-li-ath!'

> **Inside tip**
> Older children may enjoy another mode of travel! Have two people on their hands and knees and the third player can 'ride' on their backs to the finish line. Switch places for the return trip.

 One, two, stuck like glue!

Get ready...

Group size: Any
Best for ages: 5–11s
Playing time: 15 minutes
Energy level: High
Items needed: A cotton headscarf

Get set...

Aim of the game
Take two giant steps but don't get tagged with the headscarf.

Go!

How to play
Ask children to stand in a circle and number off around the circle. Choose the person whose birthday is closest to Christmas to be the

thrower and have that person stand in the centre holding the headscarf.

 **What to say**

One, two, this game's for you. One, two, here's what you do! The thrower will toss the scarf high in the air and call out a number between one and [highest number]. The player with that number will run to grab the scarf while the rest of us take two giant steps away from the centre. After two steps, you're stuck like glue to that spot! Then the person who caught the scarf takes two giant steps to get close enough to throw the scarf and tag someone with it. The tagged person becomes the next thrower. If the person who caught the scarf doesn't tag anyone, he or she becomes the thrower for the next turn.

Play until everyone has been the thrower at least once.

Radical relay

Get ready...

Group size: Any
Best for ages: 7–11s
Playing time: 15 minutes
Energy level: Medium
Items needed: The number cube, the kitchen timer and the
                balloons

Get set...

Aim of the game
Keep up the passing frenzy as you add more and more balloons.

Go!

How to play

Blow up and tie off as many balloons as there are players. Have the children form a circle on the floor and let them each roll the number cube. Tell them to remember whether their numbers are even or odd. Then set the number cube aside.

What to say

In this wild passing game, the way you pass balloons depends on whether you're an even or odd number. 'Evens' will pass balloons with their feet; 'odds' will pass balloons with their elbows. I'll start the timer, then we'll begin passing one balloon. I'll add more, so be ready! We'll see if we can have all the balloons in play before time runs out.

After the first round, vary the way evens and odds pass balloons. Use the following suggestions or let children devise their own. Pass the balloons:

❖ With little fingers
❖ Under knees
❖ Behind backs
❖ With palms of hands
❖ On fingertips
❖ Over your heads
❖ Laying down
❖ With your eyes closed

Inside tip

Young children might enjoy playing with only a few balloons and without the extra challenge of a timer.

Hot potato tag

Get ready...

Group size: 12 or more
Best for ages: 7–11s
Playing time: 15 minutes
Energy level: High
Items needed: A disc

Get set...

Aim of the game

Don't get caught holding the hot potato in this wild game of chase.

Go!

How to play

Direct children to form two rows of passengers, seated on chairs—as in an aeroplane with an aisle down the middle (see diagram). Choose one child to be the 'hot potato' and hand him or her the disc.

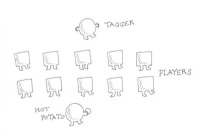

Choose another child to be the tagger. Have the hot potato and the tagger stand on opposite sides of the rows.

What to say

This is a great game of chasing and changing seats. You're on an aeroplane, and the tagger wants to tag the hot potato. They'll run around and around the seats. The hot potato can hand the disc to another player and sit in his or her seat any time. Then that player must jump up and run from the tagger before being caught. If the tagger catches you, you're the next tagger and the tagger becomes the hot potato.

If your group is very large, you may wish to play with three rows of passengers and use two discs for hot potatoes.

 # Mouse in the house

Get ready...

Group size: Any
Best for ages: 5–7s
Playing time: 15 minutes
Energy level: Medium
Items needed: The colour cube and a cotton headscarf

Get set...

Aim of the game
Pretend to be a hungry mouse and find your cheese.

Go!

How to play
Choose one player to be the 'mouse' and blindfold him or her using the headscarf. Assign the rest of the children a room of the house, such as a bedroom, living room, attic, bathroom, basement or kitchen. Make sure no two children have the same room. Instruct them to stand in the centre of the play area with their feet spread apart so that the mouse can crawl through the 'mouse holes'. Set the colour-cube 'cheese' in one room of the house between that player's feet.

I can see a hungry mouse. But there's a yummy piece of cheese in the [name of the room]. The mouse must crawl through the house to find it. If the mouse touches you, tell the mouse which room he or she is in. The mouse can keep crawling until it reaches the [name of the room] and finds the cheese.

Continue playing until each player has been the mouse.

Inside tip

For another variation, have the children scatter and sit on the floor. 'Hide' the cube on the floor and let the mouse crawl to find it as players give clues by squeaking in tiny voices when the mouse is far away and squeaking loudly as the mouse gets nearer the cheese.

 **Boomerang!**

Get ready...

Group size: Ten or more
Best for ages: 5–11s
Playing time: 15 minutes
Energy level: High
Items needed: Six discs and six cups

Get set...

Aim of the game
Be the last person 'free' in this zany game of tag.

Go!

How to play

Spread the discs and cups around the playing area as bases. You'll only need one disc or one cup for each player. (If your group is very large, ask the children to pair up.) Direct each player to stand by a base.

What to say

In this game you'll try to tag others out while you're running to a safe base. When I say 'boomerang', run to stand at another safe base. If you're touching a disc right now, you'll run to touch a cup. And if you're touching a cup, you'll run to find a disc. As you are running, you may tag others out—but don't get tagged yourself! Then, when I say 'boomerang' again, run to find another base. If you're tagged, you must sit out for the rest of the game. We'll keep swapping bases until there's only one person who hasn't been tagged.

When there's only one player left untagged, let that person choose the next game or line up first for drinks.

 **UFO**

Get ready...

Group size: Any
Best for ages: 8–11s
Playing time: 15 minutes
Energy level: Medium
Items needed: Two skipping ropes, three discs and the kitchen
                  timer

Get set...

Aim of the game
Don't get captured by the aliens!

Go!

How to play
This game is best played outdoors or in a large hall. Tie the skipping ropes together and lay them in a circle at one side of the playing field as the capture area. Choose three children to be space commanders and hand each a 'UFO' disc. (If your group is very large, use six discs.)

What to say
The flying saucers have landed and the space commanders are looking for you! I'll start the timer. The space commanders will throw their flying saucer discs like frisbees. If you're tagged by a flying disc, you must go to the capture area. If a friend sneaks over and grabs your hand, you're free to play again. See if you can keep from being tagged until time runs out. Then we'll choose three new space commanders.

Young children love this game of keeping away from the aliens. Add an extra challenge for older children by placing six cups around the playing area. Tell the children they are to snatch the cups without being tagged by a flying saucer.

Deck the tree

Get ready...

Group size: Six or more
Best for ages: 5–8s
Playing time: 15 minutes
Energy level: Medium
Items needed: Two cotton headscarves, the colour and number cubes, two skipping ropes and six discs

Get set...

Aim of the game

Be the first group of 'elves' to decorate your human Christmas tree.

Go!

How to play

Have a little fun with Christmas in July—or any month! Form two groups of 'elves' and give each group the following 'ornaments': a headscarf, a cube, a skipping rope and three discs. Let groups decide which players will be human Christmas trees first.

What to say

What a speedy group of elves I can see—and such tall Christmas trees! When I say, 'Merry Christmas', the elves will decorate the Christmas trees with their decorations. The last ornament on your tree should be the cube. Be sure to place the cube at the top of your Christmas tree. When your tree is all decorated, begin singing 'Jingle bells'. We'll see which group of elves are the quickest tree decorators.

Play until each elf has been the Christmas tree. You may wish to vary the song the children sing when their trees are decorated.

Consider ending your game time by serving candy canes or Christmas biscuits for a winning treat.

Letter-getter

Get ready...

Group size: Eight or more
Best for ages: 6–8s
Playing time: 15 minutes
Energy level: Low
Items needed: Two skipping ropes

Get set...

Aim of the game
Help your group form letters of the alphabet.

Go!

How to play
Tell the children to form two groups and hand each group a skipping rope.

What to say
You all know your alphabet very well. You've probably written each letter with crayons, markers, pencils and pens lots of times. But have you ever written letters with a rope? I'll call out a letter of the alphabet. See how quickly you can make that letter with your

skipping rope and then sit down. If your group finishes first, each group member must name a word that begins with that letter.

Continue playing until you've worked your way through the entire alphabet. As an extra challenge, have children use their bodies to form letters. Or try naming words that fit into a specific category, such as foods, children's names or animals.

 **Jolly ball**

Get ready...

Group size: Eight or more
Best for ages: 7–11s
Playing time: 15 minutes
Energy level: High
Items needed: Two skipping ropes and the foam ball

Get set...

Aim of the game
Play a cooperative game of volleyball and get the giggles.

Go!

How to play
Establish a centre line by laying the skipping ropes end to end down the middle of the playing area. Let the children form two groups and number off by threes in their groups. Tell the number ones that they'll be 'ha!', the number twos 'hee!', and the number threes 'ho!'

Volleyball is a fun game, but 'jolly ball' is even more fun! In this game, you must volley the ball three times before it goes over the skipping rope 'net'. First, number one must volley the ball to number two in your group and say 'ha!' Then number two says 'hee!' as he or she volleys the ball to number three. Then number three says 'ho!' and volleys the ball over the net to your opponents. We'll see how quickly you can keep volleying. Every time you get the ball over the net, you'll score one point. We'll play until one side has five points.

After each game, have the groups swap sides of the net. Play until one group has won two games, then let that group line up first for drinks.

Triangle dodge ball

Get ready...

Group size: Nine or more
Best for ages: 5–11s
Playing time: 15 minutes
Energy level: High
Items needed: The masking tape and the playground ball

Get set...

Aim of the game

Keep from getting tagged out in this crazy three-way game.

Go!

How to play

Mark off three sides of a triangle with six-foot lengths of masking tape. Extend the sides out a few feet for additional 'dodge space' (see diagram). Ask the children to form three groups and stand behind each of the three masking tape lines. Explain that these are goal lines and players must stay behind the lines or they are out. Designate the inside triangle as the free zone where no players may stand.

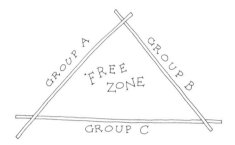

What to say

I'll bounce the ball in the free zone to begin the game. You may throw the ball at waist level or below to try to tag someone in another group. If you're tagged, you must join that group. If you catch the ball when someone else throws it, the person who threw the ball must join your group. We'll play until one group is left.

For extra dodge-ball frenzy, play with more than one ball.

> **Inside tip**
>
> If your group is very large, make a masking tape square on the floor and play fourway dodge ball. Play until there are only two groups left.

 **Seesaw tag**

Get ready...

Group size: Any
Best for ages: 5–9s
Playing time: Ten minutes
Energy level: High
Items needed: Two cotton headscarves

Get set...

Aim of the game
Join with your group to create a seesaw and then hop up and down as you try to snatch your opponents' flag.

Go!

How to play
Direct the children to number off by twos, and send groups to opposite sides of the playing area. Hand each group a headscarf and let them decide who will be the 'flag carriers'. Ask the flag carriers to tuck the headscarves in their belts or waistbands. (If they're not wearing belts or don't have waistbands, the flag carriers may hold the scarves in their hands.)

What to say
This game will get us hopping! When I say 'scatter', run around the playing area. When I say 'stop', freeze in place. The flag carriers will hop to someone in their group and take that person's hand. Then the two players will hop to another group member and take his or her hand. When you've made a seesaw by collecting all your group members, hop to your opponents and try to snatch their flag. The first seesaw that gets the flag wins.

If you play again, renumber children so that they have a chance to be with different people.

 # Noah's rainbow catch

Get ready...

Group size: Any
Best for ages: 5–7s
Playing time: 15 minutes
Energy level: High
Items needed: Two skipping ropes, a cotton headscarf and the colour cube

Get set...

Aim of the game
Make it to the rainbow without being tagged by Noah.

Go!

How to play
Tie one end of one skipping rope to the other. Lay the skipping ropes at one end of the playing area in an arch shape. Tell the children that this is the rainbow. Place the headscarf off to one side of the playing area and designate it as the 'paint pot'. Gather children at the opposite end of the playing area. Assign each player a colour (red, yellow, green or blue) and tell the children to remember their colours. Choose the child whose birthday is closest to today's date to be 'Noah' and hand him or her the colour cube.

What to say

Rainbows are beautiful, and we're going to make a pretend rainbow in our game. Noah will roll the colour cube and tell the colour. All players with that colour may walk heel to toe to the rainbow. Noah may also walk heel to toe to tag you. If Noah touches you, you must go to the paint pot (the headscarf). If you make it safely to the rainbow, stand on the rainbow until all the colours are in place. We'll see if at least one of every colour makes it to the rainbow.

Play until all the children are either in the paint pot or standing on the rainbow. Then choose another child to be Noah. You may wish to let children run, skip, hop or walk backwards to the rainbow. Make sure Noah moves in the same way to tag players. Play until each child has been Noah.

Inside tip

A different twist might be to let players who are tagged become Noahs and help tag others.

Roller racers

Get ready...

Group size: Nine or more
Best for ages: 6–11s
Playing time: 15 minutes
Energy level: Medium
Items needed: The colour and number cubes and the masking tape

Get set...

Aim of the game
Swap places in this fast-paced race—but don't get caught without a seat.

Go!

How to play
Hand one player the colour and number cubes. Give the rest of the players each a five-inch piece of masking tape. Have the children spread out around the playing area and stick their tape to the floor. Direct the children to sit on their tape. Assign the players each a colour (red, yellow, green or blue) or a number from one to four.

What to say
This is a fast-swap game. The roller will roll both the colour and number cubes and tell the colour and number rolled. The players with that colour or number will leap up and rush to swap places. The roller will try to find a vacant piece of tape, too. The player left without a piece of tape to sit on becomes the next roller.

Play until most children have been the roller.

Inside tip

This is a great rainy day game to work the wiggles out and keep children on their toes.

Row your boat

Get ready...

Group size: Six or more
Best for ages: 9–11s
Playing time: Ten minutes
Energy level: Medium
Items needed: Two cotton headscarves, six cups and two rulers

Get set...

Aim of the game
Row your boat around the buoys and back to the dock.

Go!

How to play
Place the headscarves at one end of the playing area as the 'docks'. Stagger the cups in a row down the playing area as 'buoys'. Make sure there are at least three feet between each cup. Ask the children to form two groups and think of names for their boats. Let each group of three choose a player to be the rower and hand the rower a ruler 'oar'. Tell groups to stand beside the docks.

What to say
Your boat is at the dock, but in a moment you'll head out to sea. When I say, 'row your boats', the boat members will grasp

wrists and make a boat for the rower to sit on. Then the boat and rower will paddle in and out of the buoys. When you get to the last buoy, paddle back to the dock. If at any time I shout, 'lifeboat drill!' you must quickly stop and reorganize your boat with a new rower to paddle. The first boat back to the dock wins.

Begin the game. Be sure to call out, 'lifeboat drill!' a few times during the race. Have two or three races, then let the team with the most wins choose the next game.

 **Secret word**

Get ready...

Group size: Any
Best for ages: 5–9s
Playing time: 15 minutes
Energy level: Low
Items needed: A ping-pong ball, a cotton headscarf, the foam ball, a disc, a skipping rope, a cube, a ruler, a cup and the kitchen timer

Get set...

Aim of the game
Guess the secret item before time runs out.

Go!

How to play
Set the ping-pong ball, the headscarf, the disc, the skipping rope, the foam ball, the cube and the cup in a row. Place the timer off to

one side. Help the children number off by threes and then sit in front of the items in their groups.

What to say

In this game you'll help your group figure out the secret item before time runs out. In a moment I'll ask one group to close their eyes while the other group secretly selects an item. That group will whisper the name of the item in my ear. Then we'll start the timer. You can ask questions to figure out the item such as 'Does it roll?' 'Can it bounce?' or 'Is it flat?' When you think you know what the secret item is, choose one person in your group to ask. Be careful, because you only have two chances to make a guess! See if you can figure out what the secret item is before time runs out.

After one group has chosen a secret item, swap and let the other group choose. Play until one group has successfully guessed three times.

Inside tip

For young children, try this twist. While one group hides their eyes, let the other group secretly snatch two of the items. Then let the other group guess which items are missing. Omit the timer for this version.

Balloon soccer

Get ready...

Group size: Eight or more
Best for ages: 8–11s
Playing time: 15 minutes
Energy level: High
Items needed: The balloons and two cotton headscarves

Get set...

Aim of the game
Prevent the other group from scoring by popping balloons.

Go!

How to play
Blow up and tie off a balloon for each player. Place the headscarves at opposite ends of the playing area as goal lines. Have the children number off by twos, and send groups to opposite sides of the playing area. Let each group choose a goalie. Instruct the goalies to stand beside the headscarves on the opposite side of the playing area from their group. Hand each group two balloons.

What to say
You'll really get a bang out of this soccer game! When I say 'go', begin kicking the balloons toward your goalie on the opposite side of the playing field. When the goalie gets hold of a balloon, he or she must sit on the balloon and pop it. When a balloon pops, I'll throw another one into the game. You may steal your opponents' balloons and get them to your goalie for extra points, but you can't use your hands. Only goalies may use their hands in this game. We'll keep playing until all the balloons are

popped. Then we'll count the popped balloons to see which group wins that round.

Play two rounds or until your balloons are used up.

Catapult!

Get ready...

Group size: Any
Best for ages: 7–11s
Playing time: 15 minutes
Energy level: Medium
Items needed: The balloons, two cotton headscarves, a disc and
              some water

Get set...

Aim of the game
Catapult your water balloon the farthest.

Go!

How to play
This game is best played outdoors on a hot summer day. Make sure the children are wearing swimsuits or clothes that can get wet. Make a water balloon for each player. Ask the children to form two groups and give each group a headscarf and a water balloon. Tell

the groups to decide who will be the 'catchers'. The rest of the group members will be the 'catapulters'.

 **What to say**
Let's cool off with a little fun. One group of catapulters will hold the headscarf around the edges and set the water balloon in the centre. We'll count to three, then they'll catapult the water balloon into the air and as far out in the playing field as they can. The catcher will run to catch the balloon as it comes down. If the catcher catches the balloon without it popping, we'll mark the place it was caught with a disc. Then the next group will catapult their balloon and see if they can get it to go farther without popping. On the next catapult, we'll choose a new catcher. We'll continue until everyone has been a catcher.

Be sure to pick up the balloon pieces at the end of the game.

Swivel-hop

Get ready...

Group size: Any
Best for ages: 5–9s
Playing time: 15 minutes
Energy level: Medium
Items needed: The playground ball and the kitchen timer

Get set...

Aim of the game
Swivel and hop but don't get caught! Be the last person in the line-up at the end of the game.

Go!

How to play

Form two groups. Have one group stand in the centre of the playing area. Have the other group number off by twos and line up on opposite sides of the centre group (see diagram).

What to say

This is an unusual game of dodging the ball. The players in the centre must only move in two directions—swivelling or hopping—and the moves must alternate. For example, the first time the ball is dodged, you may swivel by keeping one foot planted and swivelling around to avoid being tagged. The next time you dodge the ball, you must hop. If you're tagged, join the other group. We'll play until time runs out, and then swap places.

Play until there are only one or two players left on a side. Then begin a new game, but vary the two ways players can dodge the ball, such as stooping or standing on one foot.

London, Manchester, or round trip fare

Get ready...

Group size: Any
Best for ages: 5–11s
Playing time: 15 minutes
Energy level: High
Items needed: Two skipping ropes and two cotton headscarves

Get set...

Aim of the game
Fly your airplane and land safely at the airport.

Go!

How to play
Lay the skipping ropes in circles at opposite sides of the playing area. Designate one skipping rope as 'London' and the other as 'Manchester'. Place the headscarves at opposite ends of the playing area as refuelling airports. Choose one player to be the air-traffic controller, standing in the centre. Instruct the rest of the players to stand beside either one of the headscarves.

What to say
You're aeroplanes at refuelling airports. In a moment the air-traffic controller will call out your flight plan—London, Manchester or refuelling at another airport. Fly to that airport but don't get tagged along the way. If you're tagged, you become an air-traffic controller and help tag other aeroplanes in flight. If the controllers say, 'round trip', you must fly to each airport without getting tagged. You can't be tagged at an airport, but you

133

can only stay at any one airport for a count of five before flying on. We'll play until there's only one aeroplane left flying.

If you have a small group, remove one of the refuelling airports. You may wish to form 'jumbo jets' and let the children play in pairs.

Bridge-ridge

Get ready...

Group size: Any
Best for ages: 5–8s
Playing time: Ten minutes
Energy level: Medium
Items needed: A ruler and a cotton headscarf

Get set...

Aim of the game
Work with the entire group to plant your flag on Mars.

Go!

How to play

Tie the headscarf on to one end of the ruler to make a flag. Gather the children at one end of the playing area and give the flag to a child.

What to say

Let's pretend we're the first children on Mars, and we want to plant our flag to show we've been here. But, oh! There are lots of ridges and steep canyons to get over. The only way we'll get across Mars to plant our flag is by making a human bridge to get there. The first person will make a bridge by putting his or her hands on the floor, and then the person with the flag will hand it to someone before crawling under the bridge. Then that person will add to the bridge. The player with the flag will hand it to the next person before crawling under the bridge and so on. We'll continue handing over the flag and making the bridge until we've made it to the other side of Mars and can plant our flag.

When you've crossed the playing area, set the flag down and encourage everyone to clap and cheer. Then return to your starting place using the human bridge.

 **Juggler-jiggle**

Get ready...

Group size: Up to 13
Best for ages: 6–9s
Playing time: Ten minutes
Energy level: Medium
Item needed: The foam ball, six cups and six discs

Get set...

Aim of the game

Juggle the items in and out—but don't drop a thing or you'll drop out!

Go!

How to play

Let each person choose a playing item. Have the children form two groups facing each other two feet apart.

What to say

Not all jugglers are in the circus—we have jugglers here today! When I say 'juggle', throw your item to someone in the other line. Catch an item and toss it to someone in the opposite line. If you drop an item, you must sit out. You may catch two or three items at once, but throw them quickly to free up your hands. We'll play until there's only one juggler left.

Knot as easy as it looks!

Get ready...

Group size: Eight or more
Best for ages: 8–11s
Playing time: 15 minutes
Energy level: Medium
Item needed: The kitchen timer

Get set...

Aim of the game
Untangle yourselves and stop the timer before it runs out of time.

Go!

How to play
Ask the children to hold hands and stretch out in a line across the
playing area. Place the timer at one end of the line.

What to say
Knots in shoelaces are tough to untangle. In a moment
you'll turn into a tangly knot, too! When I say 'go', the players at
each end of the line will begin going in and out and under and
around to tie you up in knots. Don't let go of hands or the knot

will break! Then I'll set the timer. We'll see if you can untangle yourselves without breaking the knot and grab the timer before it runs out.

Older children enjoy the challenge of untangling a human knot. Choose one player to turn his or her back while the group ties itself in a whopping knot. Then set the timer and have the player try to untangle the knot before time runs out.

 Shoe dominoes

Get ready...

Group size: Any
Best for ages: 5–11s
Playing time: 15 minutes
Energy level: Low
Item needed: The kitchen timer

Get set...

Aim of the game
Find the matching shoes and place them side by side.

Go!

How to play
Direct everyone to remove one shoe and place the shoes in a 'bone pile'. Scramble the bone pile and then let each player choose a shoe (that's not their own) to wear on their hand. Set the timer where everyone can see it.

What to say

Let's play an unusual game of dominoes. I'll set the timer for two minutes. Start matching pairs of shoes by placing your hand, inside the shoe, next to a matching one that someone else is wearing. You may have to lean over someone or crawl under a player to match the shoes. We'll have a jumbled domino board when we've finished, but let's see if everyone can find a match before time runs out.

Play until time runs out or until all the shoes have been matched.

Inside tip

This is a good icebreaker game for the beginning of the year. Let the children exchange shoes and names when they've finished playing.

Index

Alphabetical index of games

Games best for younger children (5–8s)

Games best for older children (9–11s)

Games best for all ages (5–11s)

Low energy games